30 YEARS
1 MONTH
24 DAYS

JON P. BARKER

Chief Warrant Officer 4 (Retired)

CONTENTS

This book is dedicated to my sister Bonnie, a true patriot. I served with many patriots, but none more so than Bonnie. Her love of everything military was always on display, and she took immense pride in being a former military spouse, a daughter of a veteran, and the sister of three brothers who served. She was also immensely proud of her large family of veterans, including nephews, nieces, in-laws, and friends. I miss her.

Bonnie

Through it all, I have tried to keep my sanity (questionably) and not drive my wife insane. I could never have completed this work without the support of my wife Pam. Period. She never failed to be an accurate proofreader, editor, enthusiastic encourager, and the believer I needed that what I had written had a purpose. I am eternally grateful (I really am. She will get this) for her love and support. I love you.

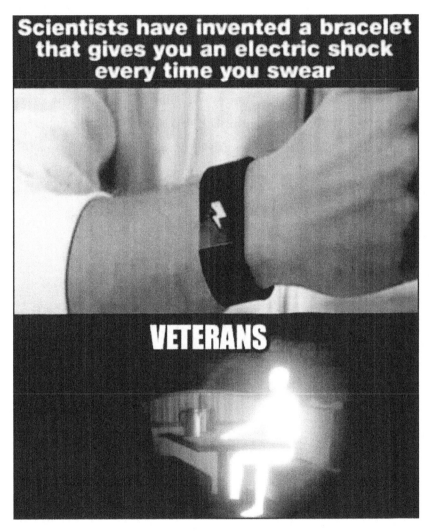

FACT...

Someone once asked General Patton why he cursed so much to his Soldiers.

He responded, "when I want my men to remember something important, to really make it stick. I give it to them doubly dirty. It may not sound nice to some bunch of little old ladies at an afternoon tea party, but it helps my soldiers to remember. You can't run an army without profanity; and it has to be eloquent profanity. An army without profanity couldn't fight its way out of a piss-soaked paper bag."

So remember this when you take offense to hearing profanity from Soldiers or Marines. We do not take the fight to the enemy and drink tea, we go to kill him and make him meet his maker.

Well said, General Patton. Patton is one of my Heroes.

MY LIFE IS BASED ON A TRUE STORY.

Just in case you were wondering.

The cover photo was taken in Iraq as AH-6 "Little Bird" helicopters from B 1/160th SOAR engaged targets. Such a cool picture.

The stories in this book reflect my recollection of events. There is no secret information divulged. Anything I have written about the units I served with is readily available from public forums such as Facebook, Google, etc. The pictures are either mine or taken from the internet. Some last names and identifying characteristics have been intentionally not used to protect the privacy of those depicted and, hopefully, to not piss too many people off. Dialogue is drawn from memory, so take it with a grain of salt, as they say. I will recount some incidents that could be considered wrong or illegal, so try and hold your judgments until the end; then, whatever you think is what you think. It is what it is or was. This is a one-time, one-of-its-kind. There will be no sequels. You only live once.

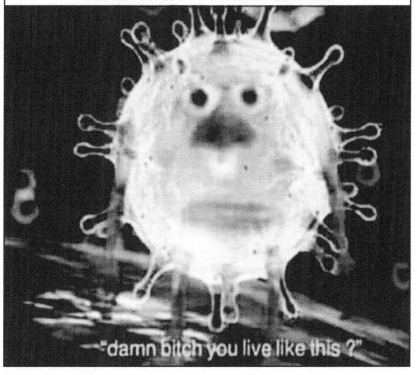

Coronavirus entering a veteran's body and finding Anthrax and Smallpox vaccines, exhaust fumes, jet fuel, hydraulic fluid, MEK, asbestos, arthritis, tinnitus, and a shitload of Motrin and alcohol

—"damn bitch you live like this?"

For 30 years, 1 month, and 24 days. MEK is methyl ethyl ketone, a fairly lethal solvent used for years by the military. We soaked parts in it. MEK is no longer allowed for use by Army personnel. Those anthrax vaccines hurt like hell.

DISCLAIMERS

- If profanity offends you. STOP.
- If politically incorrect situations and stories offend you. STOP.
- If a 30-year career in the Army has no interest for you. STOP.

You won't hurt my feelings. This book is not for everyone. If you answered "yes" to any of the three, just stop and don't waste your time.

I wrote this for my daughter Kerry so she will have an idea what I was doing for those 30 years (if I can remember). I thought it was important to document how much time I spent "On the Road," as we called our stateside deployments, and the deployments out of the country, both combat and training. I hope that one day my grandkids and their kids will read this and say, "That old fart did some shit." With that said, dates and times may not be totally accurate or in the correct sequence. Did the best I could with what memory I had remaining. I will relate those events that stand out for me over those years. Some are humorous (at least to me) and some are serious. I did a lot of stupid shit when I was young and still do. It's all part of my story.

OK, here we go.

INTRODUCTION

Attempting to put one's past in writing is a difficult task. It takes a shitload of researching, reading, collecting data, and trying to remember what, when, and where something happened. I found that while most of my memories were somewhat intact, some of them had been reformatted to fit my present-day memories. Does that make any sense at all? I have found that if you don't write shit down, you will not remember it, even seconds later. I thought about notable events throughout my life that affected me personally. The assassination of JFK (Where was I? Playing in the tobacco patch next to our house at Bald Hill, KY), the Vietnam War, and the landing on the Moon were big events, as well as the horrible death of a neighbor friend. Falling in love, getting married, and having a daughter at barely 18 years old certainly affected my teen years. I grew up quickly through necessity. Joining the Army at 19 turned out to be a lifechanging decision for sure. Tours in Germany, Korea, and Honduras opened up a new perspective on the world. Combat tours in Operations Desert Storm, Iraqi Freedom, and Enduring Freedom changed things up a bit. 911 changed us all. Retirement has its own set of challenges to be dealt with. The tanks I crewed and some of the helicopters I flew are now in museums. The Coronavirus and its spinoff variants wreaked havoc on us. Never thought I would be living through a pandemic. Such is life.

Other than a little background information about me, this book is about my 30 years of active duty with the US Army, from my enlisted time as a Tanker and Drill Sergeant to attending flight school and becoming a Warrant Officer and Army Aviator. The last section covers my time with the 160th Special Operations Aviation Regiment as both an Army Aviator and retired civilian contractor, then returning to active duty with the 160th for seven more years, hence the 30 years 1 month 24 days title. (For retirement purposes, the military counts down to the day to calculate your retirement check). Make of it what you will. I won't apologize for the level of obscenities. Just the way it was. I hope you enjoy it. Not the obscenities but the book.

1.
BEFORE THE ARMY...

I was born a poor black child. No, but I couldn't resist the opportunity to borrow one of the opening lines from the Steve Martin movie classic The Jerk (Netfix it for those too young to remember). I was actually born a poor white child in a house in Bald Hill, Kentucky, the youngest of nine children, with four brothers and four sisters. I broke the tie. Certainly not a planned child. We weren't aware we were poor, at least not when we were young. My mother and father provided us with all we needed for a safe and secure family life. My father was a veteran of WW II (World War II), serving in the Navy on LST (Landing Ship Tank) 325 and taking part in the D-Day invasion of France. LST 325 is presently the only fully operational LST remaining and is docked in Evansville, Indiana, but it still makes cruises on the Ohio, Mississippi, and other rivers. I toured LST 325 when it docked in Clarksville, Tennessee, on the Cumberland River. It was comforting to know my dad had walked those decks and slept in those bunks during WW II. He told me a lot of stories about his time on LST 325. He volunteered even though he left three young children and my mother alone in the hills of Elliot County, Kentucky. He felt it was his duty. He was that kind of man.

LST 325 at Normandy beach (I wonder if my Dad was in this picture?)

All nine of us siblings graduated high school—quite an accomplishment for my parents. My brother Garry attended Berea College in Berea, Kentucky, and was the first of us to graduate college. My twin brothers Bob and Bill went into the military after high school. Bob to the Air Force, Bill to the Navy (they wanted a choice instead of being drafted into the Army). Bill and I both retired from the military. Bill served on nuclear submarines for nearly 23 years; me, well, if you keep reading, you will see.

I guess I was always destined to be a soldier. My mom loved to talk about how I would march the local kids around. My uncle brought me a set of kid's Army fatigues that I wore out, although I do still have the shirt in my closet. Vic Morrow, "Sarge" on the TV show Combat! was my hero. We never missed a Combat! show...ever. Watched it in black-and-white since we had no color TV. (Recently, I watched a few of the Combat! reruns in color, and it seemed strange). I played Army constantly. The kids I went to grade school with would tell you I was addicted to the Army. That continued until about the

4th grade and was then replaced by whatever else a kid that age gets into. Also, around that time, my sister Carol brought home a pretty girl named Pam for a sleepover. Little did I know that when we were older, I would marry her. That's quite a story.

Me with my 1962 Ford Econoline van. (I was born in the house in the background, in Bald Hill, KY.)

This is a photo of me with my old van in which, as in the lyrics from a Lynyrd Skynyrd song, I drank enough booze to "float a battleship around" (may or may not have smoked some dope too). Had a charge account with the local bootlegger. First time I went there, when I knocked on the door, he opened it with a pistol pointed at me. Only thing I could think of to say was, "I'm Roger Barker's brother." Guess those were the magic words. Kept my bill paid up from my job at Miller's service station. Pumped gas and changed tires after school and on weekends. I visited Flemingsburg, Kentucky, in January of 2023 and purchased a 15-pack of beer legally (Fleming county is now a wet county) from a shopette built on the former site of Miller's service station. It was a strange feeling to buy beer legally in Flemingsburg. The summer of '73 I worked with my brother Roger at his autobody shop. I painted my van, but Roger did the custom artwork on the sides.

My brother Bob once loaned me his car, a 1970 Dodge Dart Swinger, while he was out of town. He tossed me the keys and said, "Total the damn thing for me. I can't afford the payments or insurance." Fastest car I have ever driven. Once had that car up to 140 mph—really stupid— the car wasn't really on the road at that speed. Anyhow, a couple of days later, I wrecked the car. Totaled it. Bob came to visit me in the hospital and said, "Thanks, man, I didn't think you'd really do it." Certainly was not intentional. Worked out for Bob, though, and in a roundabout way for me because my future wife came to the hospital with some friends to visit me, and thought I was cute.

My first car was a 1962 Dodge Dart, an ugly car, to say the least. It sat in the field next to the house with a blown engine until my Dad said, "There's a good motor in the barn. Swap out the motors, and you can have the car." I worked on that motor swap for a couple of months, learning as I went, and finally got the good motor installed. My brother Roger helped me

Me and the Green Varmit

4

get it running, and I was a car owner. The car was a puke color green, so I painted a critter on the side and named it "The Green Varmint," but it was quickly dubbed "The Green Vomit." Drove the hell out of that car until I was able to buy my van. (My brother Bill co-signed a loan for me while he was home on leave from the Navy).

In that same summer of 1973, Pam and I reconnected, fell in love, and began planning to get married. We had intended to go along with some friends who were eloping and be their witnesses, and decided, what the hell, we'll get married too. The plan was to keep it a secret until our one-year anniversary and reveal the secret at our formal wedding. Anyhow, the friends canceled, so we continued with our plan. Jumped in my old van and hit the road. Got married in a "marriage town" in Clintwood, Virginia. Got the required blood test, license, and was married by a minister in the preacher's office since their sanctuary was being remodeled. Stood in line with folks dressed in formals and blue jeans. Hit the road back to Kentucky and made it back to Mt. Sterling, Kentucky, for a wedding dinner at Long John Silvers. Went back to Flemingsburg, drove around the Dairy Queen and Whip and Sip (Or Slurp and Burp as we called it) a few times, and called it a night. We dated from then until December 9th, when we found out we were expecting a little "Firecracker" on the 4th of July. So, poor plan, poorly executed. Our baby girl Kerry was born on July 6, 1974. She became our priority. We wanted to give her all the things we never had, and being poor as could be, the military started sounding like an excellent choice (at least to me).

I made the decision to enter the military in the summer of 1975. I registered for the draft at 18, as required. The draft had ended, so it was the age of the all-volunteer Army. I was 19, married, and father to a one-year-old daughter. I had worked since graduating from high school, first at Wald Manufacturing in Maysville, Kentucky, a factory that made bicycle parts, and then at Litton Ford, a car dealer in Flemingsburg, my hometown. Wald laid me off after 179 days to avoid having to pay unemployment, which I would have qualified for at 180 days. Thanks for that, assholes. I then went to work for Litton's Ford, first as a car detailer, then as an oil changer, then as a floor mechanic. I was making about two dollars an hour and going nowhere. The military offered a solution and a way to escape. Not that small towns are bad. It just seemed to be a better place to be from than be there. I also wanted to further my education, and for a few years in the military, the GI bill would provide a way to do so.

For all of us who did. I should also add, "If I had stayed in...."

Note the cigarette and moccasins. Thought I was cool.

I had intended to join the Air Force despite my boyhood love for the Army. My brother and brother-in-law served in the Air Force and had been stationed at much cooler places than the Army choices. (Not including when they were assigned to bases in North and South Dakota, real shit assignments). My buddy Jimmy and I decided to join together. As it turned out, the Air Force had standards even back then and would not take Jimmy because he had a GED and not a high school diploma. Well, the Army recruiter was hanging out the door down the hall like a vulture; he offered to send us to Basic together with an assignment to Ft. Knox, Kentucky, plus a $2,500 bonus to be a tanker for four years. What a deal! Getting paid to blow shit up! Talked it over with Pam, and after much arguing and explaining that I would be allowed to live at home after Basic, and the Army was not a prison-type environment (which was her concept of Army life), we decided to go for it.

Shortly after that, Jimmy and I boarded a bus at Morehead headed to Louisville and the Army Induction Center for a series of tests and the required physical. We passed all that and headed to Ft. Knox on or about 28 August 1975, where I raised my hand and took the oath at the reception station at Ft. Knox on 29 August 1975, and so it began.

Jimmy and I, a few days before we raised our right hands. I intended to get my money's worth for that first haircut.

2.

BASIC TRAINING WITH C-19-5
FT. KNOX, KENTUCKY (6 WEEKS)

Casual Pay: Received a $50 cash payment called casual pay. It was purely to finance all the shit one needs to become a trainee, like shoe polish, floor wax, and basic toiletry items.

Haircut: Thought I would get a free haircut—not so much. Had to pay $3 for that haircut. My intention had been to get my free haircut and lose the shoulder-length hair I had at the time. During the haircut, the barber's break time came, so they all checked out. Guys were laughing at me, and I couldn't figure out why until I looked in the mirror. The barber had started my haircut with a few passes down the middle of my head, then quit for his break, leaving me looking like Ben Franklin. Explained the laughter.

PT (physical training): Just an excuse for the Drill Sergeants to attempt to kill us. (Not really, of course. Being in good physical conditioning is part of being a soldier.) Thought they were successful on many occasions. Got in great shape and lost a bunch of weight. PT would continue for my entire Army career.

"Here Telephone Pole!": Found out that mail call could be a humiliating experience. Failed to answer with "Here, Drill Sergeant!" loud enough when my name was called, so I was instructed to face a nearby telephone pole and yell, "Here, telephone pole!" as loud as I could. Thought it was bad, but I was soon joined by several other trainees that also failed to respond loud enough, and we were all yelling at the pole. Another time the Drill Sergeant had me low crawling under the barracks for some infraction or another—very nasty under a WW II barracks. Again, I was soon joined by other trainees who thought that was funny. Funny shit in retrospect.

Misery, Agony, and Heartbreak: Long steep hills were on each road march we went on. Damn near unbelievable that one could climb those hills with an M-16 and a ruck full of crap and whatever else was strapped to us. But like the long line of trainees before us, we did.

Later I found these hills really fun to go down in a Sheridan tank.
You could get to about 50 mph (really stupid but fun).

M-16A1 Rifle Ranges: I was the only trainee that zeroed my weapon on the first day, and I was rewarded with KP (Kitchen Police) the next day while the rest of the company returned to the range. KP sucked but did offer a chance to scavenge some extra chow. The chow sucked, but there were no other choices. I ended up qualifying as a "sharpshooter" instead of "expert" with the M-16A1 rifle due to my not listening to the instructors about how to fire the weapon. I was a country boy and had been around weapons all my life. Thought I knew all there was to know about weapons. What a dumbass! When I became a Drill Sergeant, my highest-scoring trainee was always a guy who had never fired a weapon before because he listened to the instructors.

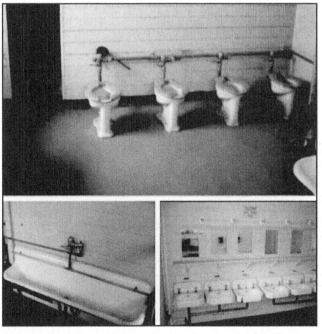

WW II barracks latrine, still in use at Ft. Knox in 1975. They sucked.

Gas Chamber: Dreaded day on the training schedule. Thought I was going to die, but I didn't. Later, as a Drill Sergeant, the gas chamber became one of my favorite days, too, so I then understood the pleasure the drills got from watching us trainees puking, blowing snot, crying, and running into trees coming out of the chamber.

End of Basic: We completed a final PT test and general soldier skills test, graduated, and was on to AIT (Advanced Individual Training).

Monthly Pay: My monthly pay was around $340. The $50 casual pay I had received was deducted from that first pay.

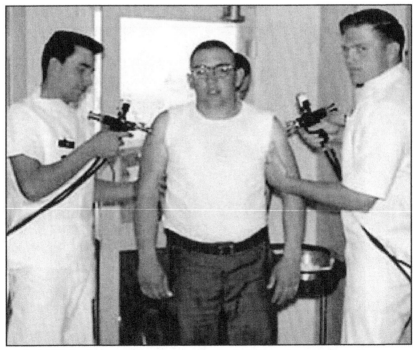

In 1975 the Army still used air guns to administer shots in mass doses to trainees. If your arm twitched, they would rip your arm open.
Doesn't the guy on the right look fucking evil?

Home from Basic for a weekend (Private E-1)

On to AIT...

.

3.

AIT WITH A-2-1, FT. KNOX, KENTUCKY 24 OCTOBER THRU 12 DECEMBER 1975

AIT was fun other than the constant pressure and testing. Had to pass all that to get the bonus. That was the goal. $2,500 would get us out of debt. We rented a house near Elizabethtown, Kentucky. AIT trainees could live at home if they were married. Not sure how we managed as well as we did, except to say my wife Pam had great skills as a budget planner and balancer as well a fantastic cook and mother. (Still is!)

First encounter with the M-60A1 tank. 52 tons of fun. Got to drive it, load it, and shoot it. Armed with a 7.62 mm (millimeter) co-axially mounted (in line with the main gun) machine gun, a 50-caliber machine gun mounted in the turret cupola, and a 105 mm main gun. Also got to shoot a .45-caliber M3 submachine gun dubbed the "Grease Gun" (it was a cheaply made weapon that resembled a grease gun but could stop a herd of elephants at about 75 feet). These were tank crewmember weapons.

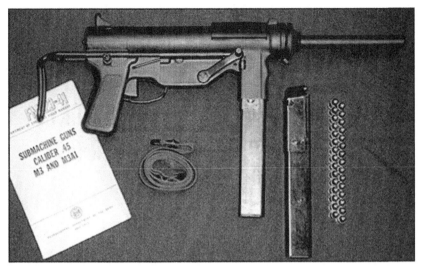

Grease Gun

Qualified Expert with an M1911A1 .45 caliber semi-automatic pistol. All tank crewmembers carry a .45. I was familiar with this pistol as my dad had one that his brother Paul used during WW II that all the Barker boys shot occasionally. (I am fortunate to still have that pistol in my possession.)

Uncle Paul was a Naval Aviator flying the PB4Y (the Navy's version of a B-24 Liberator) in the Pacific theater during WW II. He had enlisted and was trained as a radio operator, then found a program similar to the one I attended that allowed enlisted sailors to attend flight school and graduate as officers and pilots. He and his crew shot down two Japanese planes and sank the largest enemy ship ever destroyed by a land-based aircraft in the Pacific Theater, the Itsukushima Maru, a 10,000-ton Japanese tanker. He earned two Distinguished Flying Crosses. He survived the war, only to be listed as MIA (Missing in Action) in 1948 after not returning from a flight out of Kodiak, Alaska, near an area regularly patrolled by the US and Russia. He had recently completed qualification in an airborne photography system, so I always figured he was shot down by the Russians. (The US and Russia shot each other's planes down regularly in that area, but it was not publicized). Most likely, he was discovered taking photographs of something that was deemed worthy of getting shot down for, or he crashed. Found it odd that he and his crew were listed as MIA even though this occurred three years after the war had ended. My grandmother always thought that one day he would walk through the door.

Uncle Paul's .45 caliber M1911A1. Even though it says U. S. Army on it, research from Colt shows it was part of a lot of 2000 guns bought for the military, so evidently, the Navy was issued some of those. I was told several variations of how he managed to bring the pistol home.

Uncle Paul and crew five days prior to their disappearance.
He is second from right, kneeling.

AIT ended with final testing, and I managed to pass all the tests. Moved on to graduation and was awarded an MOS (Military Occupational Specialty) of 11E (Armor Crewman) and that $2,500 bonus minus $500 in taxes, of course, which I had forgotten about. Uncle Sam always gets his. Also got promoted to E-2 and was able to pin on those "Mosquito Wings," as we called the Private E-2 insignia.

UNHAPPY ABOUT YOUR LOW
WAGE? DO WHAT I DID:

* JOIN THE MILITARY
* GET YOUR G.I. BILL
* GO TO COLLEGE
* GET A BETTER FUCKING JOB!

NOBODY OWES
YOU SHIT!

Worked for me

4.

1976 THRU 1978 AT FT. KNOX, KENTUCKY

I was assigned to E Troop 2nd Squadron 6th Cavalry, a unit that had the mission of training Armor School Officers on tanks. E Troop was equipped with the M551A1 Sheridan ARAAV (Armored Reconnaissance Airborne Assault Vehicle). This was a 17-ton aluminum hulled tank from the Vietnam war intended for jungle fighting. Why the designers armed it with a 152 mm main gun is beyond me. The recoil of that damn gun would pick the tank up on its third road wheel, and then it would slam back onto the ground. Fun times. And the electrical turret—what dumbass figured an electrical turret would be good in a jungle environment? It did not work well in the humid weather of Ft. Knox, so I could not imagine how it worked in a jungle. I do know it did not work well, with testimony given by many of the Vietnam vets I worked with. First time I did gunnery in a Sheridan was quite the experience. I couldn't hit shit but still a lot of fun.

I was in the driver's compartment when a student fired a round with an object called an obturator seal not installed in the main gun breach. My first sign something was wrong was when a cloud of smoke entered the driver's compartment, and I couldn't see or breathe. We were running red lighting since it was a night shoot, so it looked like the tank was on fire. My first instinct kicked in, and I unassed out of the driver's hatch, leaving the tank running. I certainly was no hero and ran like hell to get away from that tank. A Sheridan shoots a type of paper cartridge that is extremely flammable—not good for a fire with rounds on board. The Tank Commander eventually figured out what happened and, after calming the storm a bit, went looking for me. By then, I had figured out the tank was not going to explode and was trying to get back in the driver's compartment before he figured out that I was gone. That did not happen, and I took a severe ass chewing. Deserved it.

Sheridan night firing range

Inside a Sheridan turret. The gunner sat on the right side of the main gun.

Discovered a program that would allow enlisted soldiers to attend flight school, become Warrant Officers, and fly helicopters. Sounded much better than life as a tanker. Took the test, called a FAST (Flight Aptitude Skills Test), flunked it, and was told I could never take it again. As a young dumb soldier, I believed it so removed that as a career option.

I was a Private E-2 for 13 months. I was on every shit detail in the world. Humped thousands of rounds of ammo at the Ammo Dump. If there was a detail, I was on it. Sucked. Supposedly there was a "freeze" on PFC (Private First Class). Bullshit, I thought. Who knows?

I became good friends with a couple of guys—Mike and Matt. We were in the same platoon so were on the same details most times. We also developed a habit of drinking at lunch and after work nearly every day. Beer was cheap. The dayroom (a room where everybody hung out when not working) had a beer vending machine in it. 35 cents a beer. At that time there was a policy of what was deemed a "two beers" lunch. Well, that was usually a six-pack lunch for us. Nobody cared since we were tankers and just slept it off in our tanks. I recall driving a Sheridan on a tank trail drunk as a skunk and having a grand time.

We pulled an enormous amount of guard and CQ (Charge of Quarters) duties. CQ being as a runner for the sergeant in charge. I was witness to some bizarre shit. Drugs were very prevalent at the time. I met a kid on the steps once with black residue all over his face. I knew he had been sniffing edge dressing, a black coating for the heels of our dress shoes. He was way beyond realizing that the black residue was all over his face, so when I asked him if he had been sniffing edge dressing, he denied it, which was very funny at the time. Another time, I was the CQ runner for a young Puerto Rican sergeant when a soldier came to the CQ desk and said, "I'm going to jump out a window" (He was either drunk or high). The sergeant told him he did not give a shit and go ahead and jump. When the soldier went upstairs, he logged the incident in the CQ log as "Specialist so and so say to me 'I'm going to jump out of window, I tell him go ahead and jump.'" When I read the log, I suggested he rewrite that or just leave it out, which he did. Not smart to incriminate yourself.

We pulled so much guard duty at the ammo dump that we became very complacent with the gravity of what we were there for. We would terrorize the young 2nd lieutenants performing "Officer of the Guard" by pretending to lock and load the 12-gauge shotguns we used when they approached the gate. It would pretty much make them shit their pants. Not a nice thing to do, but we thought the new "Butter Bars" deserved it (2nd lieutenant bars are yellow). That winter hit record cold temperatures at Ft. Knox, making guard duty miserable. Took 15-minute shifts walking the gate, then into the guard shack to thaw out, then back out to walk the gate.

To illustrate how poorly we were paid then, a fellow soldier had joined one of those record clubs that sent out five albums on joining, provided you sent them the shipping fees. He could not come up with the five bucks or so for the shipping, and the lack of payment would eventually result in an ass-chewing and probable judicial punishment from the 1st Sergeant. So, I wrote a check and sent it in for him in return for the albums, of course. Got me some good albums, though—ZZ Top, Rush, Kiss, Kansas, and Bad Company. I still have all five.

On 11 August 1976, I was promoted to PFC (E-3). Big day for my family and me. Pay raise! Less shit details—not so much.

At some point, I became proficient enough to perform as an "AI" (Advanced Instructor) for the Sheridan. This entailed hanging onto the outside bustle rack (storage rack) of a Sheridan turret while a bunch of untrained Armor School Lieutenants ran amok all over the tank training areas trying to learn how to effectively utilize a Sheridan tank along with other armored vehicles. This turned into quite hazardous work as they tended to seemingly try and knock you off with tree branches and anything else they could find to run into because everybody knows it's much more fun to just run over shit in a tank than go around it. Truthfully, I understood the feeling. Still do.

On 15 December 1976, I was promoted to SPC 4 (Specialist Four). Only four months' time in grade as PFC was needed to be eligible for E-4. This was a whole new world as SPC was the steppingstone to sergeant, plus another pay raise—not much for sure. At this point in my career, I was the typical Army "Spec 4." "FTA" or "Fuck the Army" was our motto. I had no intention of going beyond my four-year enlistment since I thought a career in aviation was off the books.

Along with the promotion came my first Army school beyond basic and AIT. PNCOC (Primary Non-Commissioned Officer Course). Actually, turned out to be an ok course, but not sure I learned much from it.

In August of 1976, I was part of a group that took our tanks to Louisville, Kentucky, for a display at the Kentucky State Fair. Kind of fun. Got really tired of answering questions like "Is that a CB radio antenna? and "Does it have air conditioning?" (No to both, in case you, too, were wondering.)

In the winter of 1977, there was a huge snowstorm that shut down the town and the Fort. I ran out of cigarettes the first day. Decided I was not humping a mile in a blizzard for a pack of cigarettes and just quit cold turkey. Haven't smoked since—one of the best decisions I ever made.

I also became quite proficient with the operation of the Army's jeep, the M151A2. I loved that vehicle. It would climb hills so steep I had to hang onto the front windshield so I wouldn't fall back. I have driven it through water over the hood and mud that would stop a tank. At some point, I was chosen to be the guy that drives around on the battlefield, throwing out artillery and grenade simulators, star clusters, and assorted color flares, setting off smoke pots. All this was at the direction (by radio) of the current student LT (Lieutenant) in charge of the battle for that day. This was great fun throwing out artillery simulators on unsuspecting students and, in many instances, in a place where there was no one since the student had given me incorrect coordinates. I was also able to pilfer a large quantity of these simulators and flares for myself; I guess the folks in charge figured I used them all. Would never happen in today's environment where each bullet is accounted for. I was a hit back in my hometown, throwing out artillery and grenade simulators and shooting flares. Fortunately, my parents lived in the country, so nobody cared.

M151A2 Jeep with Trailor

The photo below is of a "Headspace and Timing Gauge" used to set the headspace and timing on the M2, a .50-caliber machine gun mounted on the turret of our Sheridan tanks. (Affectionately called "Ma Deuce" by all that have operated the weapon. A really great machine gun that has been in use by the US Army since the 1930s.) If not performed correctly, the gun would not fire at the correct rate of fire and could possibly blow up, so it was important to make sure the headspace and timing are set properly. We also used this as a saying as in, "Troop, you better get your fucking headspace and timing right" when a soldier had a problem, or "Damn, that guy's headspace and timing is way off" when a soldier was not quite up to speed. I still have a headspace and timing gauge and always think about that when I see it. The shit one remembers.

Headspace and Timing Gauge for an M2 .50 caliber machine gun

I was temporarily assigned to the Engineer Board at Ft. Knox. This is where any new equipment was evaluated and approved or not. I started out as a jeep driver transporting material and people around as needed in support of the test of "The Reverse Osmosis Water Purification Unit." Shortly after the project started, one of the team members involved directly with the test was hurt in an auto accident and could not support the testing. I was then assigned to the project as one of the test members. I was given the 1700 to 0800 shift (5 pm to 8 am). Our task was to add tubes of chemicals to the water pumped from a creek into huge tanks at specified intervals and record the completion of these tasks on a ledger. It was another guy and me, and we quickly figured out that no one was coming out to check on us during this period of time. So, by 1900 (7 pm) or so, we had drunk a few beers and fallen asleep listening to music and usually slept until about an hour or so before the next shift was scheduled to arrive. We would then be sure to perform what we called "Watergating" or falsifying the records (this will only make sense to those of us around during the Nixon "Watergate" time period) to make it seem as though the entire required task had been completed. As far as I know, no one ever caught on, and the test was a huge success. Later during the first Gulf War, the units were successfully used to produce massive quantities of fresh water. So, you just never know; the shit you do may come back to haunt you.

I joined a sport parachute club on post with the intention of jumping regularly and just having fun. Learned to pack my own chute, completed all the training, and was ready for my first jump. The club used a UH-1 Huey helicopter assigned to Ft. Knox for their jumps. It was my first flight of any kind in any aircraft, and I was supposed to jump out of it. As it turned out, the weather was crappy, and we could not get the altitude required for students to jump. However, I was quite impressed with the Huey and the warrant officer pilots. Wished flying a helicopter could once again be in my future.

Later, I would travel to an airport in Indiana to make my first jump because, for some reason, the Huey was not available. It was a Cessna 172, a small airplane that required one to climb out on the aircraft's wing strut and jump from there. I was on the strut when I decided I did not want to jump from that airplane. The Jump Master would point and say, "GO!" and I would say "NO!" but finally decided it would be easier to jump than try to climb back in. So, I jumped. It was a static line jump, so I did not need to pull a ripcord. Thought I was going to die. But then the parachute opened, and all was well. As I approached the landing spot at the airfield, I tried to remember all the Jump Master's instructions about being into the wind and such. What I did not remember was how to slow your descent by pulling on the risers (cords connecting the harness to the parachute). Pulled instead on the steering toggles, increasing my descent speed. It had rained earlier, and the ground was wet. I tried to execute a PLF (Parachute Landing Fall), but my feet popped out from under me, and I landed flat on my ass, nearly driving my spine through the back of my head. Hurt like hell. I lay there for a while and finally collected my chute and walked back to the staging area. Got a good debrief from the Jump Master. Never jumped again.

I was promoted to sergeant on January 1, 1978. Finally, an NCO (Non-Commissioned Officer). This made me in charge of the guard and CQ duties. I was never sure why I was made a sergeant instead of the usual SPC 5 rank. Not much changed other than my paycheck.

I received orders to report to the 21st Replacement Battalion in Frankfort, Germany, in the spring of 1978, with a report date in June. Had hoped this would not happen with only 14 months remaining on my enlistment. By that time, I had decided I would retake the FAST test (I had researched the requirements and found no issue with having taken it before. Go figure.) and (assuming I passed it this time) apply for flight school, so we made the decision to have me do an unaccompanied tour since the accompanied tour in Germany was 36 months.

On to Germany…

.

5.
1978/79 AT MAINZ, WEST GERMANY

On arrival at the 21st Replacement Battalion, I was further assigned to the Eighth Infantry Division, then on to the 4th Battalion 69th Armor at Lee Barracks, Mainz, West Germany.

There, I was assigned to A 4/69. The unit was on a deployment when I arrived, so I was housed in a transient barracks. I attended a "Gateway" course in the German language and customs, went on my first volksmarch (a 10-kilometer walk with required checkpoints, with a medal of some kind awarded at the end—really quite fun), took a tour of the East German border, and generally just finished in processing.

My unit arrived soon, and I was assigned to an M60A1 tank crew. I did not remember much about the M-60, said so to my platoon sergeant, who immediately handed me a -10 (operator's manual) and told me to shut the fuck up and learn. I did. I was assigned as a gunner and very much enjoyed gunnery. We spent a lot of time in the field training, usually at Baumholder. Once, we traveled by deuce and a half (2-and-a-half-ton truck) to our GDP (Ground Defense Positions), designated fighting positions near the Fulda Gap, a large valley on the border with East Germany (under the control of

Communist Russia). We were expected to die there as the Russian hordes would be flooding the valley with tanks wishing to kill us as much as we did them. I doubt we would have ever made it to those positions as to get there would either require movement by rail or a road march.

We traveled by rail to Grafenwoehr or "Graf" for the yearly TCQC (Tank Crew Qualification Course). Troop trains are slow, and the lowest priority on the tracks and would be sidetracked for hours only to have a German train blow past at about 90 mph. They would then get us back on the tracks. Graf sucked. Cold as hell—generally miserable. Became a master at tank heater repair—freezing your ass off will do that. My tank qualified, as did all the battalion's tanks but one. Sucked to be that tank crew.

Absolutely!

Still proud of this. Qualifying on the Tank Firing Tables was not easy.

Railhead complete and headed for Graf. 4/69 Armor had 52 tanks assigned.
With all 52 tanks and the supporting vehicles belonging to the battalion, it
was about a 100-car train.

Sgt. Barker, Tank Commander, Baumholder training area.

In March of 1979, I was awarded my first medal, a Good Conduct Medal. This was awarded to enlisted soldiers for every three years of service without any huge fuckups in your records. Still had that one medal when I made staff sergeant. I would have that one lonely ribbon on my Class A Dress uniform until sometime around 1981 when the Army came up with some other ribbons for service, schools attended, etc. Now trainees are awarded a shit ton of medals before they even graduate Basic.

At about the six-month point into my tour, it was decided that my family would join me. Pam had told me our daughter Kerry (four years old) cried herself to sleep every night, wanting her Daddy. Couldn't have that. We borrowed money from Pam's grandmother, enough for plane tickets, an apartment, a car, etc. I rented a small (and I mean really, really small) apartment through an agency on the caserne (barracks) that made sure GIs didn't get ripped off, bought a used Audi from a GI that was leaving, and borrowed enough pots, pans, and other household items from the local GI pantry loan closet to get us through the rest of our tour. The apartment was in a part of town called Mainz Gonsenhiem. ("Party time in Gonsenhiem" was the local GI saying.) Only one person in the complex spoke English, a German girl married to a GI, but she worked and wasn't around much. Our landlord, Herr Volker, spoke as much English as we did German, so communication was difficult at best. He lived quite a distance away but came around occasionally to check on us. The military chapel we attended was a 20-minute walk, but the commissary and PX (Post Exchange) were nearly a couple of miles away—quite a long walk for Pam pushing our daughter in a stroller.

How my wife survived that tour, I don't know. I was in the field training and absent a large part of our tour. She had a four-year-old child and could not drive the car (4-speed on the column). She had no phone (life before cellphones) and had to walk pretty much everywhere. Other options were street cars or buses. She had to take the laundry to a laundromat, shop at the commissary, take my daughter to dance classes, etc., all alone in a foreign country. Absolutely impressive job!

She also had to contend with AFN (Armed Forces Network) as the only form of TV entertainment available. To say it sucked would be a compliment. Until noon they ran whatever was on the night before. Then it was slim pickings. The military commercials were laughable (and still are 40 + years later). I don't even remember the shows that aired. Pam remembers Kerry watching Sesame Street, and she had the soap General Hospital (two months behind the state-side airing). Booze, gas, cigarettes, and other items were rationed. We quickly learned how to trade with friends and the local Germans our hard liquor (I was a beer drinker. Pam didn't drink) and cigarette rations in exchange for gas rations and getting film developed from our new Minolta camera. We bought the camera at Mainz Castell for about a fourth of what it would cost in the States. Mainz Castell was in Wiesbaden across the Rhine River from Mainz. This was an impressive site consisting of acres of WW II barracks that had been converted into rooms filled with every conceivable type and brand of stereo and camera equipment. Cheap. All GIs bought huge powerful stereos. A big part of CQ duty was beating on doors and making the occupants turn down their stereos.

We damn near wore that Audi out running up and down the Rhine River Valley on weekends. We had a great time, even on a buck sergeant's pay (Called a buck Sergeant because it was the lowest of Army sergeant ranks). Visited castles and cathedrals, many over a thousand years old. Watched many fireworks displays at those castles (simulating a burning of the castle, which evidently happened to all castles at some point in history). Driving there was quite an experience. Autobahns are fun if you own a Beamer capable of 120 miles an hour. My Audi would do about 100 kilometers (80 mph) max downwind in a hurricane. Which means it did not have much power. My time on the autobahn was spent avoiding the left lane 100 mph traffic, which was not much fun. Also in Wiesbaden was a store called Verkaufs. This was surely the precursor to Walmart as they had everything in one store, a new concept at the time. We particularly enjoyed the huge fish tank. When a customer picked out the fish they wanted, someone would net it out of the tank, knock it in the head, wrap it up, and present it to the customer.

One weekend we decided to go really wild and drive to France, then through Belgium and Luxembourg back into Germany, all in one day. (This illustrates how small Europe is compared to the US. Europeans really have no concept of how big the US is. On the other hand, Americans generally have no concept of how small Europe is compared to the US. Americans also usually have no concept of how old Europe is compared to the relatively young US.) Stuffed four adults and two kids into the Audi and headed out. Toured a really beautiful cathedral in Metz, France. Headed up through Belgium and into Luxembourg. No border crossing police, no nothing until we were leaving Luxembourg back into Germany. They had a check-point set up with Luxembourg police and American MPs (military police). I was supposed to have a pass form filled out with where, when etc., approved by my Commanding Officer (CO). What I had was a form filled out by hand by me with forged signatures. The MP took a look at the form, checked out the stuffed Audi, and said, "Next time, at least type the form," and let us through. Sure he did not want to mess with all the paperwork required to arrest a couple of American GIs and their families. Lucky for us.

Seems I was always dirty and greasy in all my tanker pictures. Tanking is a dirty business. Another reason being in the sky instead of in the mud seemed like a good plan.

Deployed on "REFORGER" (Return of Forces to Germany), a yearly training event. We rail headed (loaded our tanks on railcars) to Fulda, a town near the border, then fought an imaginary battle in and around that part of Germany for about two weeks. They allowed us "free maneuver," which meant we could roam about the countryside at will running over anything we needed to as we went. It was a lot of fun maneuvering as a platoon of five tanks. The lead tank would dismount the loader to cut a fence, we would all drive through, and the trail tank would dismount a guy to try to wire it back together. We raided orchards and gardens, gathering an assortment of fruits and vegetables. At the end of the day, we would gather in a platoon defensive position and add these to C-Rats (C-rations, boxed field meals), cook them up in an empty coffee can over a tanker's stove, and usually have a surprisingly good feast. War ended at night as we had no thermal sights on our tanks back then.

A-22 Crew, left (loader), myself (gunner), right (driver), rear, TC (Tank Commander), REFORGER 1978

Me at the gunners' station of A-22. The manual turret traverse handle mount had broken and been repaired by welding, but the handle had not been remounted, thus the rusty mount by my head on the turret wall.

Sgt Barker in the driver's compartment, fixing that damn heater.

I have seen roads nearly destroyed by the 52 tanks of our battalion, along with fences and gun tubes stuck into German homes—not intentionally, but through the combination of narrow streets and careless tank commanders. I once got a three-strand fence caught in my tank's track and called the Platoon Leader to say I needed to stop and cut it out. The LT ordered me to continue. Luckily, the fence beat itself out of my track in a few miles with minor fender damage. The fear is that the wire would work its way into the road wheel seals causing the seals to leak, leading to a shit ton of maintenance and downtime. "Comrade," as we called the Germans, would put up three-strand fences to be able to claim these areas we had destroyed as fenced-in cultivated fields to claim for maneuver damage. Mo money. Don't blame them at all.

Speaking of road wheel seals, I was commanding the platoon leader's tank back from a night range when I noticed a red glow that seemed to be following me along on the left side. Well, the BCO (Battalion Commander) pulled up alongside me in a jeep and flagged me down. As I was climbing off the tank, I realized one of the road wheels on the left side was on fire—literally. I called for the driver to hand me a fire extinguisher, but when I pulled the pin and fired it at the fire, nothing. It was a common practice then among the dope smokers to remove the small screen in the extinguisher's directional horn to use in hash pipes. Unfortunately, they also tended to accidentally activate the extinguisher in the process. This was never reported, of course. So, anyhow, I put the fire out with mud off the road. The BCO began chewing my ass until I informed him it was not my tank but my platoon leader's. He took off after the platoon leader. We limped the tank back to the motor pool area, parked it, and hauled ass. (After proper documentation of the destroyed road wheel, of course.) The LT took quite an ass chewing, likely not deserved as road wheel seals tended to fail often enough through no one's fault.

Prior to a tank road march from Mainz to Baumholder, the crew and I drank several "brewskies" (beers). Illegally, of course. We did not leave until after midnight, so by that time, we were quite intoxicated. At some point somewhere on this march, I woke up and realized the tank was in the ditch, taking out the small white markers along the side of all German roads. I yelled at the driver on the tank's intercom but got no response. I dropped down into the turret and could see through the opening into the driver's compartment that the driver was sleeping. I kicked him awake, and he got the tank back up on the road. Never got a radio call or shit from anyone to say, "Hey, Alpha 22, you're in the ditch." Guess they were all asleep and drunk too. I have no idea how long we chugged along in the ditch.

After a visit from my friend Matt (he had also been assigned to Germany), Pam, Kerry, and I were driving him back to his caserne at Bad Hirschfield. I knew we would be near the border with East Germany, so I told Matt to make sure I got off at the correct exit and not go into the 1 K (Kilometer) zone. Next thing I see is a sign stating, "You are entering the 1 K zone" along with several warnings, including a "US PERSONNEL HALT" sign. Thanks for nothing, Matt. Going into the 1 K zone was bad juju. You just did not go into the 1 K zone unless you were on patrol. However, since we were already there, decided to take some pictures of the border fence and the local scenery. Went back to Mainz, figuring the MPs would be along shortly to haul my ass away. Never heard a thing about our illegal excursion into the 1 zone. Good thing. Looking back, it was a pretty cool experience for us all.

Border with East Germany (1979)

Sign marking the entrance into the 1 K zone.

The border with East Germany is heavily guarded. There are guard towers at regular intervals, and the fence is laden with anti-personnel mines, as well as the land leading up to the fence (East German side). They have ghost towns that are in sight from the border where no one lives. The lights are turned on and off, and some traffic passes through, but nobody actually lives there. In my opinion, the fence was designed to keep people in, not out. (All of this is history since the fall of the Berlin Wall in 1991 and the reunification of Germany.)

The Baader Meinhof terrorist gang was active in Germany at the time, so I found it amusing when we went to the "Post" or German Post Office to call the states (a huge pain in the ass, but the only place set up with phones dedicated to calling the US) to see that their posters would have numerous xs across the members that had been killed. Later in the second Gulf War, the same would be applied to Iraqi shitheads as they would be x'ed out as they were hunted down and killed.

Reenlisted in March of 1979 for another three years. The truth changes. Plans change. God laughs.

Motor pool guard was an experience. With the aforementioned terrorist gang at large in Germany, we had a large guard force each night. We were armed with a variety of small arms depending on who was in charge at the time. We carried M-16s, grease guns, and shotguns at various times. We had live ammo, so keeping account of that ammo was a task. I heard a couple of shots one night from the .45 caliber machine guns (grease guns) we were arming guys with at the time. I thought, *What the fuck? Shit will hit the fan now.* Never figured out why no one else seemed to care. OIC never showed up, no MPs, nothing . I have said that drugs were prevalent then. One of my guards had decided he had seen someone and shot at them. Well, he was on something, I guess. Anyhow, there was no one there, and he had not hurt anyone. I had to dig into my stash of "covertly acquired" .45 caliber bullets to replace what the dumbass had fired. I know that this sounds bad, and it was, but that was the easiest choice to avoid the shitstorm that would have happened had I reported it. Just the way it was. Don't judge me…yet.

Lucky me had CQ on New Year's night. Around 2 am, one of the soldiers living in the barracks came staggering down the hall with a huge gash on his head. Guess there had been a drunken fight, and one of the guys had clocked him with a bunk adapter (a steel pipe used to assemble the cheap Army bunks in the barracks). I knew this was gonna get ugly, so I called the MPs. The MPs arrived and hauled off the hurt soldier as well as the accused bunk adapter assaulter. Quite a night. Sometimes on CQ, I would get a call from the SDO (Staff Duty Officer) that he was coming to the barracks for surprise room inspections. This was code for he was trying to catch someone smoking dope. I would alert the barracks. I know. I should not have done that. The SDO would usually have me meet him at the entrance to the barracks and have me posted outside, positioned so I could see anyone tossing dope out a window (our company barracks was on the second floor). Occasionally that would happen, but I never reported it to the SDO. It would have been just a huge pain in the ass and was not worth it.

Received orders assigning me back to Ft. Knox. Sold the Audi to a GI for what I paid for it, and in August 1979, we boarded an airliner in Frankfurt and headed back to Kentucky. It had been an incredibly special time. We just didn't realize it.

Entrance to Lee Barracks, Mainz, West Germany

Back to Ft Knox...

6.

1979-1981 AT FT. KNOX, KENTUCKY

I was assigned to E Company 2nd Battalion 1st Armor Training Brigade as a tank instructor. Not a bad job but not particularly challenging. It was in my best interest to apply for Drill Sergeant School. This would stabilize me for two years with a third-year option. The turnaround for tankers was about 18 months stateside, then a tour of Germany or Korea. By then, I had decided I would retake the FAST test for flight school and just let the chips fall as they may, as they say. But in the meantime, I applied for and was accepted into Drill Sergeant School.

Drill Sergeant School at the time was a self-paced school. I know it sounds ridiculous. We were required to memorize the Drill and Ceremonies (D&C) Manual as well as the PT Manual. Made it through the school without much drama and was awarded the 3X MOS Identifier and was qualified to wear the Drill Sergeant Hat, or "Round Brown," as they were called, along with the Drill Sergeant Badge, or "Pumpkin." Also, a $50 a month "Pro Pay" (proficiency pay) for the 15-hour days and putting up with cycle after cycle of dumbass trainees. The pay started at $50 a month for the first year, $75 a month for the second year, and $100 a month for an optional third year. Returned to E Company, now as a Drill Sergeant.

Ours was an OSUT (One Station Unit Training) Company, which meant we put our trainees through six weeks of basic training, then eight weeks of AIT. That's a long time to put up with the same bunch of dumbass trainees. I once went through three consecutive cycles without a high school graduate. No shit. In the world of the all-volunteer Army, the standards were drastically reduced to fill the ranks. No wonder we were called "DATS" (Dumbass Tankers). Remember, this was 1980 and 81.

I was a sergeant (E-5) Drill Sergeant working with staff sergeants (E-6) and sergeant first classes (E-7). Guess who gave all the PT instruction, D&C instruction, and any other instruction they did not want to do? That's right—the buck sergeant drill.

I must admit that I once beat the shit out of a trainee. Really bad judgment on my part. The trainee in question refused to perform his guard duty assignment. We used 2.5-ton trucks ("Deuce and a Half" to us) to haul around the trainees to their various guard posts. When said trainee refused his guard posting, I emptied the truck and had a trainee drive us to a secluded location. I jumped in the back of the truck, removed my Drill Sergeant hat, and proceeded to beat the hell out of that trainee. I'm guessing he was intimidated by my being his Drill Sergeant, or I might have taken an ass-whooping instead. Anyhow, said trainee returned to duty and completed his guard duty posting (I don't remember having any more issues with that trainee). Another time I should have gone to jail, I reckon, but it was immensely satisfying in a weird way. I was not going to let a trainee refuse my orders. Period. Not happening on my watch. Different times back then, you could get away with a lot. Good thing.

Drill Sergeant Barker (sergeant E-5), still wearing that one lonely ribbon. The hash mark on the left sleeve designated every three years of service.

Cartoon drawn by one of my trainees

The curled walking stick I'm carrying in the cartoon above is nicknamed "Mr. Root." My trainees hated Mr. Root. It served many purposes, such as encouraging a slow-moving trainee to move faster (how I accomplished that, I'll leave to your imagination) or serving as a weight when placed on outstretched forearms. (Really a form of trainee torture. Try it once, and you'll understand.) Mr. Root went on all road marches with me. I still have Mr. Root.

Had this one trainee we called Brasso for reasons to be explained. His family had sent him one of those bottles with a knitted animal over it. He hated Black folks, so when he was around with the bottle, a couple of our Black drills would take the bottle from him and hold it and caress it and just fuck with the kid. Brasso would nearly cry. This sounded mean and I guess it was, but some trainees would try just about anything to get kicked out of the Army. We became immune to it after a while.

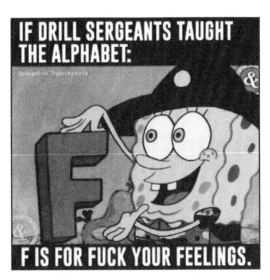

We were not there to be nice.

Brasso came in one morning and said he had swallowed an entire bottle of aspirin. Called the ambulance, and they hauled him away. Found out later that they pumped his stomach. Sent him back to the unit with a counsel at unit level slip. Did so. Next day he came in again and claimed to have taken another bottle of aspirin. Repeat of the previous day with another counsel at unit level slip. Counseled again. Next day he shows up claiming to have drunk Brasso (Brasso is a harsh liquid polish used to shine brass and other things.). Well, by this time, I was tired of his shit, so I said show me, never thinking he had actually drunk the stuff. He disappeared, then reappeared with a can of Brasso, said, "Watch this, Drill Sergeant," and went ahead and drank a good amount of Brasso. I said, "OK, you're a fuckin nut case. You win," and called the ambulance. This time they figured he was indeed mentally unstable and kept him. Later, they sent him back to the unit to out-process for a nut case discharge. Finally got him sent on his way back to civilian life.

I had my trainees running on the PT track. One trainee was slow, and I thought he was just being lazy. I told him he better run until he died. A couple of laps later, he collapsed on the track. Stuffed an amyl nitrate capsule up his nose (all the drills had amyl nitrate capsules taped inside our Round Browns) with no apparent reaction. Bad shit when one does not react to an amyl nitrate capsule up the nose. Called for an ambulance and figured I was going to jail. He returned to the unit in a few days for out-processing for a medical discharge. He had a heart condition that he was unaware of that became clear when under physical stress.

Speaking of undiagnosed conditions and stress, had several trainees have epileptic seizures. Usually in the mess hall (dining facility), and usually with a full tray of food. The trainee would drop the tray, hit the floor, most likely bash their teeth and face into the floor and begin to flop around like a fish out of water. Very scary shit. I would direct a few trainees to pile on top of him and hold him down amongst the blood and food. It was quite a mess. On all occasions, they were returned for medical discharge processing, having never known they were epileptic until they were subjected to stressful situations. I learned to judge a fake collapse from the real thing rather easily. If the trainee bashed his face, it was real 100 percent of the time. If the trainee jumped up and ran after an amyl nitrate capsule up the nose, he was most likely faking.

And then there were these two trainees (twins) from West Virginia—dumb as a box of rocks. Great kids. Ask them to move a mountain, and they would do it; just don't ask them to write a report on it. In an attempt to be discharged, one of them (one was smarter than the other) claimed to have taken the academic test to enter the Army for the other one and wanted me to kick them out of the Army. I kicked them out of my office instead and told them they would continue with training. At the end of training, one brother failed the end-of-cycle test requiring a retest after further training. The other brother refused to leave until that happened. I was not going to separate the two. I allowed the smarter brother to live in the barracks (illegally) and hoped the dumber one would pass on the retest. He did, and they went on their way back to the West Virginia National Guard. I'm sure they were successful there.

I was subject to two congressional investigations. These are when a trainee or the trainee's parents call their congressman to report what they considered unusually harsh treatment. One was when I entered a barracks room occupied by "holdovers," or shitheads who had failed to pass or complete training. It was after a weekend, and the room was a total mess. Pizza boxes lying around, soda cans, and trash all over. I pretty much lost it and overturned the trash cans, threw the lids at the sleeping shitheads, and called them all a bunch of worthless fucking pieces of shit among other things. They got the message.

The second congressional had something to do with my so-called use of excessive PT to enforce standards. Each time I was called before the CO, he would ask me if the alleged incidents had occurred, and both times I lied my ass off and replied, "No, sir, you know me better than that." Fortunately, the CO understood that I was lying and chose not to sacrifice my career for punk-ass trainees with connected relatives. That happened in both cases. Never heard a word from either of those investigations. Good Commander. Saved my ass.

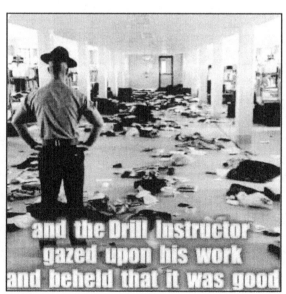

A Marine drill in the pic, but you get the idea. That shit was fun.

Drill Sergeants monitor their trainees' mail. All packages were opened in front of Drills to ensure no bogus materials were inside, such as alcohol or tobacco. Cookies and other sweets were required to be shared with the rest of the trainees. Suspicious mail would be opened in my presence also. One trainee received a letter that I was positive contained what appeared to be a large doobie (marijuana cigarette for anyone unfamiliar). When called in to open the letter, the trainee immediately began to deny any wrongdoing, even before the letter was opened. I took the trainee into the latrine and had him open the letter, which did indeed have a large doobie inside. After fucking with the trainee for a while about calling the MPs and jail time and such, I had him flush it down the commode and ended it with a warning to ensure that no more doobies be sent to him. He nearly cried, watching it swirl away. He was a good trainee, and nothing good would have come from pressing charges against him.

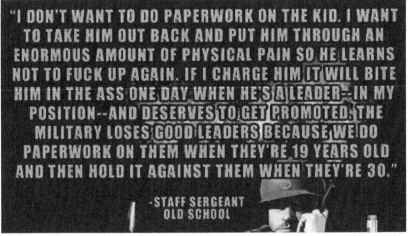

"I DON'T WANT TO DO PAPERWORK ON THE KID. I WANT TO TAKE HIM OUT BACK AND PUT HIM THROUGH AN ENORMOUS AMOUNT OF PHYSICAL PAIN SO HE LEARNS NOT TO FUCK UP AGAIN. IF I CHARGE HIM IT WILL BITE HIM IN THE ASS ONE DAY WHEN HE'S A LEADER--IN MY POSITION--AND DESERVES TO GET PROMOTED. THE MILITARY LOSES GOOD LEADERS BECAUSE WE DO PAPERWORK ON THEM WHEN THEY'RE 19 YEARS OLD AND THEN HOLD IT AGAINST THEM WHEN THEY'RE 30."

-STAFF SERGEANT OLD SCHOOL

This is so true. This concept was applied to me a few times throughout my career, and I have applied it a few times myself and never regretted it.

Twice I had to escort trainees to the brig (jail) at Ft. Knox. Both times I was required to draw a .45 pistol and use a vehicle from the motor pool with a driver to escort those trainees to the brig. The charges against them were fairly minor, an AWOL (absent without leave), and an assault. The assault charge was the result of the trainee hitting another trainee in the head with an empty ammo can (used to store shoe polish and floor wax). They had both been sentenced to jail time as part of their punishment. Holy shit! I thought us drills treated trainees badly, but nothing like what I witnessed from the MP guards. Sure as hell made a believer out of me. They slapped those trainees around a bit, and I just braced the wall and got the hell out of the way. Don't ever want to end up in a military jail. Just hell no!

When pulling CQ duties, one of the requirements was to check the mess hall. I never quite figured out why, but it was quite an experience to sneak into the place and turn on the lights. It was like a horror movie when thousands of roaches would retreat away from the light. A moving carpet of roaches. Really entertaining on a long night.

At some point, we shut down E Company and moved to A Company. Not sure why they shut E down; money, I would guess. So, now I was a Drill Sergeant in the same company and barracks where I had attended AIT as a Private. Small world, or small Army, I should say.

I attended BNCOC (Basic Non-Commissioned Officer Course) in January 1980 as a Buck Sergeant. Again, I was with NCOs that out-ranked me in this class. Not that it mattered. I made the Commandant's List (Top 10 Students) anyhow, and it was basically a waste of time school for me. I enjoyed the gunnery phase since I got to do gunnery in a Sheridan, which I hadn't gotten to do for some time.

The movie *Stripes* was filmed at Ft. Knox while I was a Drill. If you watch it, you will see guys issuing clothing to the trainees. I knew those guys well. They used our motor pool (place where we parked our tanks and other vehicles) for some scenes, as well as many other locations in Ft. Knox. They hired some Drills to march troops around and conduct PT and D&C (drill and ceremony) for them to film. They paid them well and fed them donuts and coffee. I had just picked up a new cycle of trainees and could not get away. Too bad. Love that movie.

"Arrrmy training, Sir!" scene from *Stripes*.
All the wooden barracks are gone now.

We had a psycho SGM (Brigade Sergeant Major) while I was a Drill Sergeant. I don't know; maybe his Vietnam experiences had overcome his rational thinking. Guess we'd call it PTSD (Post Traumatic Stress Disorder) now. He would actually low crawl (hands and knees, folks) up to a ground-level window in the barracks, trying to catch guys asleep on duty. Guy was seriously fucking nuts. Never caught me asleep on CQ just by luck. Hell, everybody slept on CQ duty occasionally.

We had completed the day's training early for once. We had three Drills assigned to our platoon, which just never happened. Anyhow, we had left the short straw Drill with the platoon that afternoon and met at the bowling hall for a beer before heading home. In walked the Brigade SGM (the same psycho one). We mistakenly thought he would join us for a beer. Instead, the asshole asked who had given us permission to take off from work. Being the dumbass I have always been, I replied, "No one, Sergeant Major, " and explained we were done with training, so I decided to grab a beer on the way home. Fuckhead never said a word, but the next day I was called into the CO's office and formally charged with Article 15 (bad, career-ending judicial shit) for drinking on duty. Not the other guy—just me. This went on for a few days until one of the Drills that outranked me stood up and swore that he had given me the time off. What a great guy. Charges were dropped. Could have been a career-ender.

Along the way, I managed to complete a couple of college classes, but the long hours and late nights did not jive with classes, so I was a C student. Should have done better.

Promoted to Staff Sergeant on August 1, 1980. The promotion board had been a joke. I was a Buck Sergeant Drill Sergeant. Think they would have promoted me if I had shown up drunk. Had to chase down my promotion orders. Found them in an inbox of some paper pusher. This would become a theme for me later—chasing down paperwork.

I once again took the FAST test. Did really well. Never heard from the "you can never take it again" Nazis. Proceeded with the flight physical and sent it off to Ft. Rucker, Alabama. Had my required interview with a Senior Flight Officer—an old CW4 (Chief Warrant Officer 4). He asked me why I wanted to become a pilot when the likelihood of dying was high (he was a Vietnam vet). I did not have a good answer for that, but it didn't scare me either.

There was a stagnant time when I didn't hear anything from anyone. Returned to the CW4 that had interviewed me looking for answers, and he informed me I had done well on the flight school board, had been accepted, and had a school date. Holy shit! Went looking for those orders and found them again in some paper-pusher's inbox. Luckily, I still had time to decline a third year of Drill Sergeant status and extend my enlistment so I could complete flight school.

During this time, Pam was able to get the first two years of pre-nursing college completed at the University of Kentucky Extension of the Community College in Elizabethtown, Kentucky—a milestone for her.

Being a Drill Sergeant turned out to be one of the most satisfying jobs I ever held in the Army. I would like to believe I produced well-trained soldiers. I never had so much power and respect in my life, including later as a Chief Warrant Officer Four.

So, I was headed to Warrant Officer Flight Training. Said goodbye to my fellow Drills and headed for Ft. Rucker, Alabama. Little did I know just how demanding this course of instruction would be on my family and me, and another chapter in my Army career began.

On to Ft. Rucker...

7.
FLIGHT SCHOOL AT FT RUCKER, AL, 1982

I was assigned to the 60th Company for WOCMD (Warrant Officer Candidate Military Development), usually shortened to WOCD. Started off as a "Snowbird," a student that had not begun training. Was issued the WOC (Warrant Officer Candidate) Guide, a pamphlet that I would later realize was the WOC bible. It contained all the instructions for maintaining our "cubicles" as required to meet the TAC (Training and Counseling) officers' standards. Should have taken the time then and memorized that damn manual. Snowbirds performed administrative crap and shit details. I was further assigned to class 82-10, "Gray Flight."

Warrant Officer Candidate Barker with his wife, Pam WOCMD,
60th Company (6 weeks)

March 1 was the official start of training and began with the ritual "Black Day." It began around 2 am with the TACs coming in, raising hell, and generally harassing all candidates. This was followed by PT, a log drill, and just about anything else they could think of to make us miserable. They were successful. They destroyed any attempts we had made to have our cubicles ready, along with our wall lockers and barracks. I don't remember what else we were subjected

64

to that day, but it was a long day. Regular days started with wake-up at 0430 followed by PT. We had seven minutes to make our bunks, get dressed, and whatever else you had to do. You learn to get a lot done in seven minutes. I once woke up early and decided, what the fuck, I'm getting up. Bad decision, as one of the TAC officers walked by and asked what I was doing up. In a momentary lapse of reason (shout out to the Pink Floyd album), I answered, "What's it look like I'm doing?" Wrong answer. "Pink slipped" (a pink form that we were required to carry at all times where fuckups would be recorded and demerits documented) and awarded a boatload of demerits.

Ate my first "square meal," requiring the food to be picked up with a fork, raised to mouth level, and then moved to the mouth to deposit the food while looking straight ahead. The fork was then returned to the plate by the same square route. No talking was allowed while eating (unless "pig rights", another story, had been earned). I was sitting across from a guy who would later become a close friend, and we eventually lost it and spat peas and began laughing. Not cool. The TACs were on us like stink on shit and immediately pulled our pink slips to reward us with demerits. Back to "pig rights." Pig rights referred to the right to talk while eating and not be required to eat "square meals." This right was usually earned through some really ridiculous "pranks." "Gray Flight" pranks were anything from putting the commander in a baby bib to eat his meal with a baby fork and spoon to serenading our TAC with a Christmas song in 90-degree weather. Pretty lame. Gray flight did not earn many pig rights in WOCD.

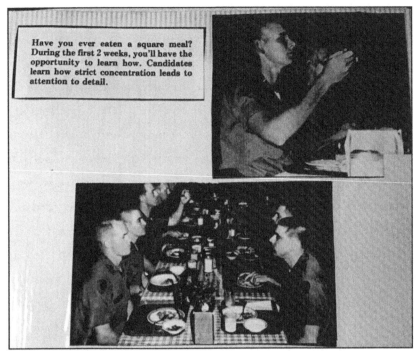

Have you ever eaten a square meal? During the first 2 weeks, you'll have the opportunity to learn how. Candidates learn how strict concentration leads to attention to detail.

Square meals sucked. I never learned shit from eating square meals.
We ate square meals during all of WOCD.

Demerits were awarded to enforce standards and added to each candidate's weekly cumulative score. The lower your score, the better. I had seriously high scores at the beginning of training. Also, "military letters" were required to be written to explain your deficiencies and how you were correcting them. I wrote military letters every night. Earned more demerits from mistakes on the military letters.

MILITARY LETTER

1. All military letters will be done on 8"x10½", white or yellow, lined paper; unless the letter is being typed, in which case it will be done on 8"x10½", white, unlined, bond paper. If a military letter is typed, it will be in accordance with AR 340-15.

2. The format below will be followed for all types of military letters.

DEPARTMENT OF THE ARMY
60TH COMPANY, 6TH BATTALION
FORT RUCKER, ALABAMA   36362
(skip three lines)

ATZQ-AB-OS-A   1 August 1979
(skip one line)
SUBJECT: List briefly the subject of your letter; e.g., Pink Slip
(skip three lines)

THRU: TAC Officer
        60th Company, 6th Battalion
        Fort Rucker, Alabama 36362
(skip three lines)

TO: Commander
        60th Company, 6th Battalion
        Fort Rucker, Alabama 36362
(skip four lines)

1. List your request or deficiencies in complete sentences in the first paragraph.
(skip one line)
2. List or state why you had this request or deficiency in complete sentences in the second paragraph.
(skip one line)
3. State what you are doing to correct the deficiency in complete sentences.
(skip one line)
(If you are at the end of the first page, you must leave at least two lines at the bottom; then you will start the second page with the first usable line. Second and subsequent pages will be numbered, centered and 8 lines down from the top of paper. (Heading on second and subsequent pages as follows.)

ATZQ-AB-OS-A   1 August 1979
SUBJECT: The same as on the first page
(skip one line)
4. List other related information.
(skip four lines)

                              (signature)
                              JOHN DOE
                              SSN 123-45-6789
                              WOC Class 79-00

Military Letter Format Example (I hated those fucking Military Letters)

APPENDIX J
DISCREPANCY-DEMERIT GUIDE

Code Numbers for
Marking Weekly In-
spection Report
and Report of

Observation	Description	Demerits
0	Needs improvement. (Effort has been made.)	0
1	Not aligned. (Ruler placed against alignment does not touch all items.)	1
2	Not neat (e.g., wrinkled, loosely rolled, lettered sloppily, strings).	1
3	Not evenly spaced (e.g. hangers in locker uneven).	1
4	Not as prescribed (e.g., towel folder backwards, socks in wrong sequence).	1
5	Unbuttoned, unzipped, unsnapped.	1
6	Dusty (e.g. finger accumulates dust when ran across surface).	1
7	Dirty. (Accumulation other than dust, e.g., grass, soap, lint, or greases.)	2
8	Not shined. (Reflection obstructed by fingerprints, scuffs, etc.)	2
9	Not properly maintained. (Unserviceable condition, e.g., buttons missing, light bulbs burned out, leaking faucet unreported.)	2
10	Hidden article (e.g., cigarette butt, paper, sock in pocket, drawer, boot).	2
11	Inattention. (Failure to make timely correction.)	2
12	Improper marking (not marked IAW Standardization Guide).	2

DISCREPANCY-DEMERIT GUIDE (Continued)

Code Numbers for Marking Weekly Inspection Report and Report of Observation	Description	Demerits
13	Not marked. (IAW Standardization Guide.)	3
14	Rusty (e.g., razor, polish can).	3
15	Abuse. (Unauthorized use of issued item; e.g., using Army blanket to polish floor.)	3
16	Not displayed. (Unless explained on discrepancy card.)	3
17	Failure to secure property (any item not under lock; also unlocked security locker).	10
18	Failure to follow instructions.	10
19	Failure to supervise.	10
20	Not prepared for inspection (e.g., display in disarray, etc.)	10
21	Failure to respond to correction.	10
22	Quibbling. (Argumentative attempt to impose a trivial distinction or objection of no significance to evade the point.)	15
23	Flagrant neglect. (No significant effort made.)	15
None	Public use of obscenity.	*
None	Improper personal hygiene (failure to brush teeth, etc.)	*

WOC Guide Demerit List (there were two more pages). The demerits would balloon, as in code numbers 2,7,18, and 23, for one offense. Number 23, Flagrant Neglect, seemed to always get added to my demerits. 200 plus demerits a day was normal for me. The ones with no demerit score were grounds for set-back or elimination.

Pam was allowed to see my cubicle once on a wives' tour and accidentally brushed my ash tray, knocking it out of alignment. She then touched the ashtray, trying to realign it, and left a fingerprint on it. For this offense, I accumulated the above-mentioned code numbers totaling 30 demerits. She later tried to explain what had happened to my TAC officer, but to no avail. Number 23, Flagrant Neglect, was, of course, added to my deficiencies.

"Taxi time" was assigned for more serious offenses, consisting of putting on the dress green uniform and marching up and down the street in front of the barracks for a period of time decided by your TAC (minimum of one hour). Taxi time was completed after regular training, so the time you needed to get ready for the next day's inspection and study was gone. Did more than my share of taxi time. Between the massive demerits, taxi time, military letters, and all the other bullshit one had to get done, I don't know how I managed to get through WOCD.

Part of my problem was the fact that I had just come off Drill Sergeant status and was now the "fuckee" instead of the "fucker." I was a staff sergeant, and most of the candidates were PFC or specialists, with a few "high school to flight school "guys. Academically, I was fine. I did not see the point in rolling my underwear into a rockhard 7-inch roll that could be used as a weapon. I did not see the importance of ensuring I had no fingerprints on an ash tray that was never used but had to be exactly aligned with the corner of the desk. I was having a tough time adjusting. Finally, I wound up on Senior TAC Probation. This is where WOCs that are not performing to standard are assigned to either improve or be eliminated. I improved. At some point, I finally got it—just play the game.

The real reason for all that nonsense was to teach attention to detail. The pre-flight of a helicopter is critical, as well as all other preparations before the skids leave the ground. "Take-offs are optional, landing is mandatory" is a motto I learned to live by. It's too late to correct anything once the skids leave the ground.

Speaking of mottos, the WOC motto was "A candidate will not lie, cheat, steal or tolerate those who do." We quickly changed the last to "tolerate those who get caught," at least among ourselves. "Static items" or hidden items that were not subject to inspection, like a tube of toothpaste or a shoe polish container, were strictly prohibited. A few Gray Flight candidates were caught with said static items hidden in the ceiling of the barracks. They were "set back," meaning they would restart training at Black Day and be reassigned to the flight behind gray, Orange Flight. Pretty harsh punishment, but this was considered an integrity violation, very bad in WOC-land.

Being an ex-Drill Sergeant, I volunteered to lead all the PT instruction (not because I was a volunteer; it was just less painful to do it myself). I also did the majority of marching the flight around to classes and whatever. The TACs did not care for my Drill Sergeant badge. Not sure if it was jealously or what.

As I was dealing with the life of a candidate, poor Pam was dealing with the life of the "social leader." We had been selected to be the flight social leaders at the beginning of WOCD, but as a candidate, I was busy trying to survive WOCMD while Pam was entrenched in the duties of the flight social leader pretty much solo. She was dealing with a few whining candidate wives, rank-conscious wives of the 60th company, and generally was subjected to a constant barrage of requests and requirements. Everything she had to do was

71

accomplished through hours and hours on the phone, going to meetings, and driving from place to place, as there were no computers, email, or cell phones available. She did have a few great Gray Flight wives who gave her much-needed cooperation and support. She managed all this remarkably well, which is why she was personally chosen by the 60th and 61st company commanders' wives for this duty. I just happened to be her husband, who was along for the ride.

We were allowed a one-hour visit with family on Wednesday evenings. Not much time to catch up. On Sundays, we were allowed to meet our families at church, then ride to the mess hall, where they could join us for lunch. After that, we could visit until 3 pm in the Warrior lounge (AKA "roach lounge" due to the large roaches living there. Alabama had some big-ass roaches). Most of that time was spent shining brass and shoes.

Every two weeks was the Friday beer call in the Warrior lounge, a chance to unwind and just have a good time. Each flight was required to put on a skit of some kind. To us, they were ridiculously funny, probably due to the large quantities of alcoholic beverages consumed. A favorite for us all was when the Brigade Commander would come down to party with us. The guy was just a hoot—very foul-mouthed and down to earth. I think he really enjoyed hanging out with us candidates. One Friday, they allowed our wives to attend (the only time in WOC history). Not sure why, but that never happened again. Not politically correct, I think. The wives enjoyed it, however.

We had to complete "peer ratings" each week where each candidate would rate their peers on such qualities as leadership, dependability, and so forth. We called them "peer rapings." I was always well-rated except for "tact." Guess I was lacking a bit of tact. Still do.

We completed WOCD on 9 April, and became Gray Flight 82-25, and headed to 61st Company where the real challenges would begin.

Graduation from WOCMD cake

On to 61st Company...

61ˢᵗ Company (10 weeks)

Primary flight training. We were issued those oh-so-cool flight suits, sunglasses, and flight gear. We began academics and prepared to begin flight training.

I began the first part of flight training on a particularly low note. First day on the flight line, I was pink-slipped for not knowing an EP (emergency procedure). EPs are committed to memory and are never allowed to be wrong when babbled out to the IPs (instructor pilots). EPs became a sleep aid for Pam while quizzing me every night. Well, I had not mastered that quite yet, being DAY ONE on the flight line. Even that did not suppress my extreme delight with my "nickel ride" or first flight in a TH-55A Osage helicopter. What a blast! This began my love for flight.

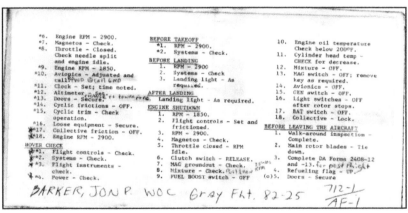

My TH-55A checklist

The Gray Flight wives made these for us. The nickels were the year of each candidate's birth. The wives from each flight made something unique for the candidates to commemorate their "nickel ride."

The TH-55 was not an easy helicopter to learn to fly, especially learning to hover. Imagine using both hands and both feet to control a mechanical mass of spinning hardware while making radio calls and receiving instruction from your IP. I thought I was crashing many times only to be saved by my crusty old IP, a civilian contractor. Once I mastered the art of hovering, the rest was fairly easy.

Pretty much explains it. PFM (pure fucking magic).

Autorotations are hard to explain. When the motor quits on a helicopter, quick physical reactions are needed, or you will crash. One must immediately lower the collective (a stick used by the left hand to control the throttle and pitch in the helicopter blades); apply aft cyclic (the center stick used to control forward, aft, and sideward motion); place the helicopter in trim with the pedals; adjust airspeed; adjust rotor speed as required; pick a place to land; make a Mayday call; try not to shit your pants (at any point in this process) and pray it turns out well. At the bottom of the autorotation or just prior to touchdown, another series of actions must be perfectly performed, or again, you will most likely crash. A very intense 30 seconds or so. I learned to complete a successful autorotation quite well.

Around the ten-flight hour point, my IP climbed out of the helicopter and sent me on my way solo. Three trips around the traffic pattern without fucking up are required to have successfully soloed. Solo is a defining point in flight school. This means you are competent enough to fly alone to and from stage fields (large airfields used to train students) and train in the traffic pattern alone, hopefully, without damaging the helicopter, yourself, or anyone else. Really the big deal was sewing the solo wings onto that gray hat, designating you as one who had completed his solo flight. We never realized just how close to killing ourselves we were during this period of training. It is a testimony to the IPs training that we did not.

TH-55As at a stage field

Rear view of a TH-55A helicopter on the ramp at Hanchey Army heliport. The traffic pattern looked like a swarm of bees when students and IPs were departing to and arriving from stage fields.

The main rotor blades were engaged by extending an actuator that tightened six belts (like fan belts on a car, only thicker). The joke was "rubber bands kept the rotor blades turning"—not so far from the truth. No automatic anything on the TH-55. Manual throttle, no hydraulics, a 4-cylinder, 180 hp aviation gasoline engine, and maximum airspeed of 75 knots (86 mph).

My solo certificate

The last WOC to solo in each flight was required to ride the "solo cycle" (a modified bicycle with rotors attached) down the street in front of the barracks while being drenched with beer from your own flight and the flights with you in primary. A ritual since stopped; not sure why. Probably a part of the same process that would later make WOCs WO1 Warrant Officers upon completion of WOCMD. That I certainly agree with. No need to be treated like a piece of shit candidate for ten months while trying to learn how to fly a helicopter. We just endured it.

WOC riding the solo cycle

Each Friday evening, all the flights competed in a tug-of-war battle. Gray flight was great at tug of war. Why is this important? It earned us pig rights. We never lost a tug of war and enjoyed pig rights all through primary.

We attended training at the altitude chamber during this phase. I remember my friend Jeff and I having a great time trying to perform some simple tasks prior to passing out; lack of oxygen will kill you, just what the chamber is designed to teach.

"George" was the nickname for the over-speed reduction built into the helicopter's engine to prevent damage to the engine from improper throttle manipulation. I learned to expect George often due to my lack of skills. When George kicked in, it would cause the helicopter to violently yaw about if the throttle was not immediately reduced. As previously said, we were a millisecond from killing ourselves most of the time. We just didn't know it. That's how you learn. The final check ride was administered by an IP that you had not flown with to ensure fairness. I did really well. My first AQC (Aircraft Qualification Course) completed.

We were allowed to live at home on weekends during this phase, provided your academics were good, and you were progressing on the flight line. I always earned this privilege but spent most of my weekends studying because nothing came easy for me.

Pam continued to shoulder the burden of being Flight Social Leaders. She planned all social activities, including luncheons and parties, and headed up bake sales, where the candidates' wives would show up outside classroom buildings with various sweets for us ravenous candidates to buy and eat during breaks. The food rules were off during bake sales, so we all took advantage of this to ingest mass quantities of whatever they presented. When I looked at the paperwork and logistics required for those bake sales, my wife went above and beyond to ensure they were successful.

All the phases were completed by successfully passing a "phase inspection." This was a dress greens inspection by a TAC officer of your wall locker and living space. I passed the inspection. Every phase began with a "phase party," in this case, a cocktail party at the Officers' Club coordinated by Pam.

On to 62nd Company…

62nd Company (24 weeks)

Gray Flight entered the junior phase at the beginning of this training. This was indicated by an orange tab attached to our name tags. We were allowed to live at home if married, a huge plus for this phase.

We started our UH-1H Huey qualification. At the time, the Huey seemed like a Cadillac compared to the TH-55. It is a very forgiving helicopter, and I don't remember anyone having a problem completing the AQC.

UH-1H Huey. The orange doors are a Rucker thing advising all that a student pilot is operating this helicopter. (Beware!)

At the completion of the AQC, we began BI (basic instruments). For those not familiar, this requires flying the helicopter without visual reference outside the cockpit, a skill needed when flying in IMC (instrument meteorological conditions, or "in the clouds"). Correct interpretation of the instruments mounted in the dash of the cockpit kept you upright and flying. Navigating along the airways was much like flying on airborne interstate highways with checkpoints that usually required actions of some sort, such as a radio call, altitude change, or beginning an approach. The skills to do this are difficult to learn, to say the least. This was a dreaded part of training due to the substantial number of setbacks and eliminations. The Huey simulator was ok, but by today's standards a really antiquated piece of crap. I was not particularly good at instruments, especially in the simulator. My "stick buddy," Jeff, was exceptionally good, so I was the challenge for my poor IP. I flunked my first check ride in the simulator, which was a requirement to progress to "AI" (advanced instruments). I was totally devastated. The recheck was in a few days after some added training with my IP. I did ok on the recheck. We lost several members of our flight to the Huey simulator; some set back, and a few eliminated. We moved on to AI, which was all in the aircraft. I was much better in the aircraft and completed instrument training with no further issues.

UH-1H Instrument Simulator (I still hate that damn thing)

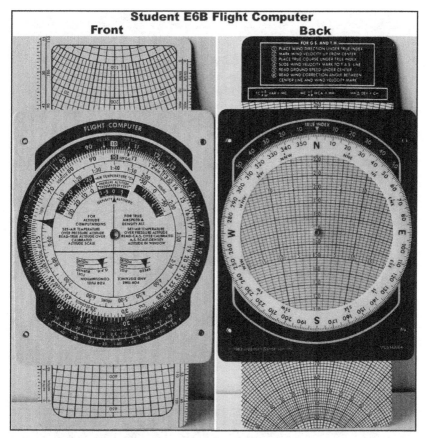

Front and back of the 1982 version of a manual flight computer we called "The Whiz Wheel." Now performed by on-board computers with these functions built into the software. I hope they still teach this, as computers have been known to crash...

The E6B flight computer: so easy even Spock could use it.

Along the way was the also dreaded weather class. This was another part of training that historically ended with several students set back or eliminated. Studied my ass off and made it through ok. I have not explained that we had a half day of classes and a half day of flight line on the aircraft. If either got behind in any way, you were eliminated or set back. The weather class was a six-week course of instruction—very intense training. It took time in the real world to understand the weather folks were mostly "weather guessers," and the decision to fly or not was yours and yours only.

Sometime during all this, Pam and I were required to attend a reception at the Commanding General's residence. Not a problem usually, but the invitation stated casual dress was allowed. Well, to me, casual was, well, casual—no tie. Against my wife's advice, I went without a tie. I was at once rounded up by my TAC Officer prior to the receiving line, received an ass chewing, and sent home to retrieve a tie. Lesson learned: always wear a tie if in doubt or have one available. I should have listened to Pam since she had taught protocol classes and knew the proper dress.

At the completion of this phase of training, we moved on to the senior phase. Thank God! We now sported a black tab with our nametags. We were allowed to join the Officer's Club and generally left on our own to complete training. The senior phase party was held at our TAC officer's house with a Halloween theme as it was, well, October. This event was also planned by Pam, same as were all the flights' social activities. It was a great party.

Most of Gray Flight moved on to Huey Combat Skills training. Some of us, likely due to a higher academic standing, were selected for "Aeroscout" training, involving an OH-58A Kiowa Scout helicopter AQC and another grueling round of academics. Lucky us. We began with the aircraft AQC, which was difficult for me. I had problems with my IP, a CW2 who was a lazy dirt bag. I was not progressing well. Finally, I was evaluated through what was called a "Prog (Progression) Ride" administered by the Senior IP, or SIP

(Standardization IP). At the completion of this check ride, he said, "You don't have any issues; you just need a new IP," and assigned me to another IP. I still had a difficult time but progressed normally with the new IP. That SIP probably saved my ass. Sometimes it takes an IP change. I remember that in my Drill Sergeant days, we would sometimes transfer poor-performing trainees from one Drill to another and usually were successful in completing that trainee's training. Sometimes it just takes a new set of eyes.

The final check ride was tough, but I did ok because I was well-trained and had studied my ass off, something I did every day of flight school. I still remember the relief I felt to be finished. Words cannot adequately describe it. This was the most incredibly challenging course of instruction I had/have ever attended. I cannot ever describe the pressure put on a WOC in flight school. I was truly blessed to complete the training without a setback. I was not a gifted student nor pilot, and that made every phase extremely hard. I literally worked and studied every moment I could. I would spend hours upon hours in my study room relentlessly studying the shit ton of material we had to know and be evaluated on. Well, it paid off in the end.

We transitioned to nights and NVGs (night vision goggles). We wore full-faced goggles. Imagine wearing a set of blinders and losing a great deal of your depth perception; the outside world is green with at best 20/50 vision. We performed low-level and normal touchdown autorotations wearing those, which now seems really dumb. One of the maneuvers I performed required a 50-foot hover with a 360-degree turn. At the end of that turn, I usually was lucky to still be in my lane, later realizing my IP had the same limitations, so he would be as lost in space as I was. For whatever reason, I slipped effortlessly into nights and NVGs. Thank God something came naturally for me. We were one of the first flights to complete NVG training in flight school, a ten-flight hour qualification.

Full-faced AN/PVS-5 NVGs (designed for ground use). With these strapped to your face, your narrow field of vision was a blurry green. We used tape or Velcro to attach weights to the back of our helmets to offset the weight of the goggles. Still made your neck hurt. The only way to see the instruments in the dash was to focus one tube inside the cockpit. Today's goggles are lightweight and far superior to this version.

OH-58A last preflight on fly-by day. Fly-by day was just prior to graduation when the Gray Flight students piloted a formation of Hueys and Kiowas over the parade field on Ft. Rucker, where the families would be able to enjoy their WOCs' last flight in flight school. Since discontinued. Not sure why.

Me in an OH-58 in formation during Gray Flight's "fly-by." Pam circled me.

What a gaggle. The last two Hueys had smoke generators they turned
on as the fly-by ended.

I had received orders sending me to Ft. Knox flying Hueys as a
"medivac" (Medical Evacuation) pilot. We were elated with this since
we had left from there to attend flight school. About three weeks before graduation, I received another set of orders assigning me to Ft.
Lewis, Washington. As in Washington State. Quite a difference. This
would require a 3,000 or so mile drive and radically changed all our
plans. Welcome to Army Aviation.

The Ft. Rucker Officers Club had a display of each flights progression consisting of a wooden pyramid with the different color hats moving up as flights graduated. It was a big deal to watch your hat move up. Finally, the gray hat was at the top!

Most days I thought this would never happen.

We were promoted to WO1s a day before actual graduation. Pam was allowed to pin my bars along with the Brigade Commander since we had endured the social leader duties successfully. Most social leaders were replaced several times throughout the months of training, but we managed to complete flight school as social leaders from start to finish. Again, entirely due to Pam's inherent people skills, leadership, and plain old hard work.

Pam and the Brigade Commander pinning on my WO-1 bars

Pam, me, and Kerry after promotion to WO1 ceremony.

Three happy campers.

And it was not over. The graduation ball was a huge amount of paperwork, coordination, and generally a pain in the ass. Pam again managed to make it come off without a glitch. She, along with the other wives, received their "gradumate" diplomas and a set of miniature wings during the graduation ceremony. Pam's mother, Jewell, sister Rhonda, my mother, Loval, and sister, Bonnie, were able to make it down from Kentucky. It was nice to have some of our family attend.

CONGRATULATIONS AND BEST WISHES FOR A REWARDING CAREER

WARRANT OFFICER CLASS 82-25 — Members of Warrant Officer Rotary Wing Aviator Class 82-25 who graduated Wednesday (Dec. 15), from the nine-month flight training course at Fort Rucker (Ala.) are, kneeling, from the left, Warrant Officers, W-1, Andre J.P. Dube, Terrence A. Zultak, David O. Pigeon, Thomas W. Gerrish, Jerry R. Litton, and Raul Carillo. First row standing are, from the left, Warrant Officers, W-1, Richard J. Potter, Steven W. Lindsey (Distinguished Graduate), Jeffrey S. Sears (Honor Graduate), James D. Kay, Don D. Allen, William E. Yeager (Commandant's List), Jeffery G. Fagan, Ramon C. Manriquez, and Jon P. Baker (Class Leader). Second row are, from the left, Warrant Officers, W-1, Guadalupe Saldana, Randall E. Talley (Honor Graduate), James D. Whitney, James L. Bryan, Patrick G. Furlong, Stanley L. Wicker, James L. Albert Jr., Jerry D. Embry, Craig K. Witt, Paul W. Rauscher and Richard R. Fell. Third row, from left, are Warrant Officers, W-1 Ronald L. Arsenault Jr., Paul L. Godwin (Honor Graduate and Leadership Award), Oswald B. Ingraham, Brooks M. Catrell, John O. Brewer, Roderick D. Davis, David S. Rutledge (Honor Graduate), Michael W. Spaulding (Commandant's List), Lester F. Dehr III, and David C. Moore. Not available was Warrant Officer, W-1, Scott F. Williams. *(U.S. Army Photo)*

Spelled my last name wrong—as usual. If I didn't answer to Baker, I would still be in a waiting room somewhere.

Jeff, me, and Butch showing off our new Army Aviator wings.

Had one final run in with a TAC Officer. This guy was, I guess, jealous of my Drill Sergeant Badge. He told me I was no longer allowed to wear the badge as a warrant officer. I knew better, having researched the wear of the badge. I told him I had orders designating that I was allowed permanent wear of the badge, I was not removing it, and that, basically, he could kiss my WO1 ass. I vacated the area rapidly before things got out of hand. Luckily for me, there is really no rank among warrant officers, so we don't salute each other or pay much attention to who outranks whom. Good riddance, Ft. Rucker.

It was all a game. Top right is my original solo wings. The gray hat fell apart long ago. The Hoverbug card was presented by my primary IP.

On to Ft. Lewis, Washington…let the real fun begin.

8.

1983 TO 1986 AT FT LEWIS, WASHINGTON

Arrived at Ft. Lewis in January of 1983. Lived for six months in a really nice apartment in Lacey, Washington, about 15 miles from Ft. Lewis. Pam and I really liked Lacey but hated Washington with it's rain and fog. And more rain. Our daughter Kerry, on the other hand, loved it. She had started school in the third grade with a great teacher, Mr. Kiekafer, or "Mr. K," as he was called. Later Kerry would become a teacher with the married name "Kilcoyne," so she became "Mrs. K." When she and Mr. Kiekafer reconnected later in life, they had a laugh about that. Moved into quarters on Ft. Lewis after about six months. This was our first and only experience with military quarters, and we liked them.

Decided we could continue to hate this place or embrace it and the rain, so we did. Learned to love it and accept rain as an everyday event, much like Germany, in fact. Everyone kept telling us about a majestic mountain to the east that was so beautiful, and when it finally did appear, it was. Mt. Rainier dominated the scenery when it was not foggy and raining.

View of Mt. Rainier from our quarters

My first flight at Ft. Lewis was an orientation flight in an AH-1S Cobra helicopter (a tandem-seat Attack Helicopter). I really enjoyed the flight even though the PIC (Pilot in Command) tried to make me sick looking through the gun sights not knowing I had many hours looking through tank sights while on the move. I logged quite a few Cobra hours over the years. Not a lot of flights were available in an OH-58 during that time as there was a shortage of money for flight hours and parts for the Kiowa, the cheapest helicopter in the Army inventory to fly, so how does that make sense?

My night orientation flight was in an OH-58A. We flew up to Seattle right through downtown. Absolutely gorgeous at night. Right past the Space Needle. I was in awe. What a great flight!

Most of the flights I did get were across the Cascade Mountains to the desert to train at the Yakima Firing Center. We flew through passes in the Cascades to get to Yakima to avoid flying at higher altitudes and crappy weather. I have never flown over more beautiful terrain. Breathtaking. Those flights are still a highlight of my time at Ft. Lewis. I saw elk, bears, mountain goats, eagles; every flight was an adventure.

If the weather was really crappy, we would take the southern route, which took us through the Columbia River Gorge. Another breathtaking flight over just awe-inspiring sights. Never tired of that flight either.

Made several flights to Mt. Saint Helens (A volcano that erupted in May of 1980). Being young dumbasses, we flew inside the blown-out part of the mountain to get a look at the new dome that was building inside. The actual devastation from the eruption was still very clear. Spirit Lake was still so full of trees one could walk across it. The trees for about 25 or so miles around the mountain had been blown down as if they were toothpicks in a perfect arrangement waiting to be scooped up for delivery. I had never seen such a display of formidable power. Even though it was several years after the eruption, we had to perform a special engine wash on our helicopter engines due to the corrosive ash. Occasionally, we would find a light coat of ash on everything from the mini eruptions from Mt. St Helens.

Aviators are progressed through three levels of training called RL (readiness level) 3, 2, and 1, 1 being the highest level of readiness and training. I progressed normally and was considered ready for my PIC check ride once I reached the RL1 level. I passed my PIC ride around the six-month point at Ft Lewis. As PIC, I was in charge of my helicopter, which was a big deal. Being a PIC meant I was solely responsible for those who strapped in with me as well as the helicopter.

I was returning from a mission and had flown into night conditions at Yakima—not good since we were not using NVGs at the time. I flew to where I was certain our bivouac area (the area where our tents were) was and found the guys had put out a "Y," a lighted Y-shaped set of lights. I was elated since this gave me something to reference on the ground that I was familiar with. As I neared the ground, I noticed the Y was moving about and realized it was a bunch of guys holding "bean bag lights," or lights using batteries attached to sand-filled bags. Never was more pleased to shoot an approach to a "living Y" than that night. Fortunately, one of our senior aviators went the extra mile to do that for me and get me safely on the ground. Thanks, Ted!

We flew up to Moses Lake Airport to eat dinner and return to our field site under night conditions. We justified this as training, and it was. (Any time spent in the cockpit flying, talking, and navigating is valuable training, and you have to eat.) No goggles. We were a flight of 3 OH-58s and 3 AH-1 Cobras. Upon arrival back at our training site at Yakima, it was total chaos. There was no moon and no artificial illumination since this was a tactical landing area. It was blacker than four feet up a bull's ass. We had a general idea where to land, but no reference to the ground. There is an old saying that I referenced earlier. "Take-offs are optional, landing is mandatory." Given a choice, I would have flown until daylight rather than attempt a landing. Not enough fuel, so landing was mandatory. It was fucking dark. The plan was to set up an approach and hope to see the ground before impact and make a controlled landing. We were successful. Ended up scattered all over the place. One of the Cobras blew down a tent. I had to hover about a quarter mile to our designated landing area—not fun, but better than the terrain impact option. What a goat screw. Another time, I took off after dark to conduct a flight to put time on the helicopter to put it in the window so that required maintenance could be performed the next day. All was cool until my radar altimeter suddenly indicated 50 feet. Even though I knew I was above the ridgelines, I about shit my pants and pulled maximum power to begin a steep climb to avoid hitting a mountain. I climbed until I knew I was above any mountains in the area. I think I may have been able to see the lights of Seattle. I mean, I really climbed. It scared the fuck out of me. The crew chief in the left seat never said a word, and I didn't either. I'm sure he thought I had lost my mind. Turned out my radar altimeter had malfunctioned. Good times.

The 268th began NVG training (NVG flight was still new to most Army aviation units), so the next progression was NVG PIC. This happened while we were on a trip to Yakima. We were still using full-face goggles then, which is having a set of NVGs strapped to your face, drastically reducing your field of vision, requiring a constant scanning technique developed during many NVG flight hours. The NVG world is green, and the depth perception is poor at best, with the aforementioned visual acuity being about 20-50, which really sucks. I successfully passed my NVG PIC ride, another big moment in my Aviator progression. Went on to become a "UT" (unit trainer), which meant I helped the IPs instruct pilots in NVG flight. Got me a lot of NVG flight time.

Worked with some Airforce A-10s (Close Ground Support Fixed Wing Aircraft, which is kickass in the right hands). What a bunch of egotistical shitheads. Worst bunch of people I have ever worked with. Showed up at the flight briefing wearing scarves, looking like the Red Baron, and believe it or not, their flight leader was named Lance Beam. I can't make this shit up. Not a good training event.

Also worked with a group of Air National Guard Pilots flying A-7 Jets at Yakima. Such professional guys. Give those guys a heading and target description, and they were on it. I was hovering on top of a ridge at Yakima, and one of the guys topped the ridge about 100 feet from me, belly-rolled the aircraft over the ridge, and continued to the target. Absolutely impressive! Vastly different from their egotistical A-10 counterparts.

One day on a flight in Yakima—go figure—upon take-off, I heard a whishing sound--not one of the usual sounds. Landed immediately and rolled the throttle to idle—no sound. Returned the throttle to full open and took off. The weird whishing sound again. Landed and shut down the helicopter. As the rotor spooled down, I spotted something on one of the rotor blades. Turns out the guy I was flying with had tossed a foil candy bar wrapper out the window (it was winter, so we had doors on), and it stuck to one of the main rotor blades. Amazing how much noise is generated by a candy bar wrapper. When in doubt, land and figure it out. Saved my ass more than once.

This is a picture of what we called the "edge of the world" at the Yakima Firing Center, where it borders the Columbia River. It was great fun to take new guys and hover up near the edge, then suddenly dive off, usually scaring the hell out of them, just as it did me my first time.

Deployed to Ft. Bliss, Texas, to take part in Border Star, an annual training exercise. One night we departed our bivouac area to conduct an NVG training flight around the area. It was another of those no-illumination, black-ass nights. I was in lead, and at the second check point, I spotted a couple of aircraft ahead of me that came out of no-where. Began to make calls to my flight to alert them and discovered those were my Cobras that either missed the checkpoint or turned early, or something. I called bullshit on training that night, and we headed back to base and landed. Live to fight another day, another motto I had adopted.

In 1983, I was part of a flight from Ft. Lewis to Amarillo, Texas, to turn in our OH-58As for conversion to the C model, a much-improved version. We flew over Crater Lake in Oregon, an extinct volcano filled with water, at about 50 feet AWL (above water level). Very stupid. We spent a night in Las Vegas just because we could. Flew over the Hoover Dam and the Grand Canyon. Seeing the USA from a helicopter is just different. Later in 1983, I would later make the same flight from Amarillo to Ft. Lewis in the new C Model and pretty much did the same dumb shit in reverse.

I was promoted to CW2 on 14 December 1984. Nothing significant about it except another pay raise—always welcome.

Promoted to CW2 by the 268th Battalion Commander, with Pam and Kerry.

My Commander promoting me in this picture was then LTC (Lieutenant Colonel) David Hicks. He often chose me to be his pilot during training at Yakima. We spent many eight-hour days in the cockpit together. Pam and I became good friends with him and his wife, Jonti. He rose to Brigadier General before his retirement.

Good man. good friend. Not common between a W1/W2 and a Lieutenant Colonel. We recently drove to Florida to say a sad good-bye as he passed away after a long illness.

I climbed Mt Rainier on 16 June 1985. It was quite a challenge even though I was in excellent physical condition and had taken a day of mountain climbing training the weekend prior to learning how to use an ice axe and crampons (spiked shoes strapped to boots). Spent a night at a basecamp at 10,000 feet and began the climb to the top at 2 am to the 14,410-foot summit. The view from the summit is spectacular. The lack of oxygen was apparent. Every few steps required a rest, and it seemed as if I was walking through waist-deep mud. Quite an experience.

Summit of Mt Rainier at 14,410 feet. We each carried a beer and our flight school hats. Someone carried the C Company Guidon. It was cold as hell up there, so I don't know why those guys had their shirts off.

I applied for and was accepted into the MTP (Maintenance Test Pilot) school at Ft. Eustis, Virginia. MTPs fly aircraft to ensure safe and airworthy aircraft are released for flight after maintenance or to troubleshoot and figure out what is wrong with the aircraft. I have always had a knack for fixing broken mechanical issues on automobiles and whatever. Figured I could apply this to helicopters as well. Plus, those guys always got flight time because helicopters break regularly. Lots of moving parts.

In July of 1985, I departed for Ft. Eustis to attend Phase I of AMOC (Aircraft Maintenance Officers Course). It was extremely boring. This part of the course was to train students in the administrative part of maintenance. Necessary but boring. Managed to graduate on the Commandant's List for that portion of the course.

Phase II was the aircraft flight and academic portion. Kicked my ass. Required committing the Test Flight Checklist to memory. Why would one need to memorize a checklist? Good question. In a single-pilot aircraft, while conducting in-flight checks, one cannot let go of the controls to consult the checklist. Helicopters always require the pilot to be on the controls, at least the type I was flying back then that had no autopilot or stabilization systems. Thus, the requirement to memorize the checklist. There was also a requirement to complete troubleshooting problems with the aircraft systems—again from memory. My MTFE (Maintenance Test Pilot Flight Evaluator) liked to play hangman with us students. Each wrong answer built another leg in the gallows. I was hung most days. Made it through Phase II in November of 1985.

In May of 1986, I applied for and traveled to Ft. Campbell, Kentucky, to assess for the Night Stalkers, an elite Special Operations

Aviation Unit. It was what I wanted to do as an Army Aviator. Failed at what was a brutal assessment. They told me to apply again when I had more experience. Absolutely the right call; just didn't know it at the time.

I was enrolled in the Warrant Officer Advanced Course through correspondence. Back then, they would send you study booklets with a test at the end of the book; the test would then be completed and sent in for evaluation. We, the Warrant Officers enrolled in the course, would, upon achieving a passing score, supply the answers to our compadres enrolled in the course. I kept my booklets piled in the bathroom of our quarters, so basically, I completed nearly all of the advanced course on the shitter. Well, it was a bullshit course.

I completed several college courses through the Embry Riddle Aeronautical University (ERAU) satellite campus in Ft. Lewis. Not a particularly great student, but I passed enough courses to come within reach of an Associate Degree.

Got a call one day from the DA (Department of the Army) Warrant Officer Division. The guy offered me a Black Hawk transition plus the MTP course follow-on. I knew this was leading to something. I had been at Ft. Lewis for over three years, so I expected I would get orders for somewhere soon. So, the catch was a year assignment to Korea. Not that I could turn it down.

Pam decided she and Kerry would move back to our hometown in Kentucky for the year I was in Korea. Her plan was to put her nursing career to use in one of the local hospitals, but she would first need to get a Kentucky nursing license. Kerry was already upset that I would be gone for a year, so when Pam mentioned that she would be working, Kerry said, "Mom, I'm so proud of you for being a nurse, but with Daddy in Korea and you working all the time I won't have either one of you." That was when Pam decided to be a stay-at-home mom. Families always pay the price. Also, during my tour at Ft. Lewis, Pam was an "Acting Commander's Wife" for three single C Company Commanders, with all the responsibilities and duties that came with it. The 268th Commander's wife and the other company commanders' wives selected her despite having other higher ranking officer's wives assigned to C company. She was well trained for the job after our stint as social leaders in flight school and always carried out the job magnificently, even when attending one of the most difficult nursing schools in the country.

I decided I would use a home base program which guaranteed return assignment to Ft. Campbell, Kentucky, after my Korea tour. We traveled back to our hometown and rented my sister's house. I headed off to "Mother Rucker" for the Black Hawk AQC. Completed the AQC on 12 November 1986 and headed back to Ft. Eustis for the Black Hawk MTP course. The Blackhawk MTP course was not too bad since I knew the drill about memorizing the checklist, although the academics were challenging due to the complexity of the Black Hawk helicopter. Completed the MTP course on 18 December and headed to Korea in January of 1987.

On to Korea…

9.
1987 IN KOREA

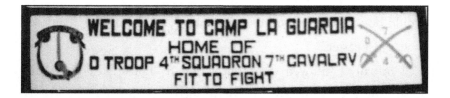

Korea was a 12-month unaccompanied tour. I was assigned to the 2nd Infantry Division, D Troop 4th Squadron 7th Cavalry, Uijongbu, Korea. That's right, "Custer's Cav." The compound I was assigned to was Camp LaGuardia, and the airfield was LaGuardia Airfield. I lived in a barracks we called Alcatraz, a condemned wooden building. The good thing about that was if one had the desire to knock a hole in the wall, no one cared (also, no one fixed it). I roomed with a guy named Jeff. We immediately hit it off and became close friends. Jeff was an OH-58 MTP, so we had much in common and spent long days on the flight line together. We also partied pretty hard.

The "Ville" outside the fence had many bars that catered to GIs. On my second night, Jeff abandoned me in a bar, so when it came time to head back to the barracks, I flagged down a taxi. I had been told that if you become lost, a taxi would always take you to what we called "Jackson Circle," a street outside Camp LaGuardia. The taxi driver was not pleased with my request for some reason, so I finally just got in and insisted he take me to Jackson Circle. He took off, went around a corner, and about another 50 feet to Jackson Circle. I felt like a complete jackass. Tipped him and headed to Alcatraz. There was a midnight curfew in effect for E-6 and below. The gates into our compound were guarded by Koreans, so we would often sneak our enlisted compadres through the back gate after midnight after bribes were doled out to the guards. I got to the point where I would buy a bottle of booze once a month for the back-gate guards. It was just easier.

I initially employed the services of our "house boy," Mr. Kim. Extremely cheap for what he performed. He did laundry, shined boots, and cleaned Alcatraz as best as he could. Found out that about 90 percent of male Koreans were known as Mr. Kim. Sadly, Mr. Kim passed away during my tour to be replaced by Mr. Kim. The best yaki mondeau (fried pork dumplings) in the Ville could be had at Mr. Kim's shop. Mr. Kim tailored a suit I had made fashioned straight out of a Sears catalog. All different Mr. Kims.

One of the first initiations into the "Cav" was called a "carrier qual." This entailed running around the floor in the Officers' Club or "Sabre Lounge" while being sprayed with water from fire extinguishers and doused with beer until one was cleared for an approach, then up steps to launch your body down the bar which was slick with soap, water, and beer. A bell hung at the end of the bar, so the object was to complete a carrier landing, have the landing approved by the senior aviator in the unit, then, after the third successful landing, ring the bell. This was usually performed while quite shit-faced. You just had to be there. I successfully completed my carrier qual.

In the pattern for "carrier landing qual."
My friend Van said I looked like a beached whale.

I made UH-60 PIC and MTP quickly. Another qual that took longer was the "border qual." This was needed to fly the border trace between North and South Korea. Crossing into North Korea would be very bad shit (As in they would shoot your ass down bad shit. Had a Cobra get shot at while I was there). Completed my border qual and "Papa 73" qual (Papa 73 was the airspace and helicopter routes around Seoul).

Had the misfortune to draw the short straw for pay officer duties. Back then, soldiers had the option of being paid in cash. I signed out a .38 caliber pistol and six rounds, and the soldier that accompanied me drew an M-16 rifle with one 20-round magazine. We drove to Seoul to pick up the money. So here are me and another soldier in an Army truck with about $40,000 in cash in a brown paper bag, armed with a pistol and a rifle, driving from Seoul back to LaGuardia to disperse payday cash for the soldiers. I was thinking, *What a stupid fucking plan.* Stupid plan executed in reverse to return cash not dispersed.

In the fall of 1987 took part in "Team Spirit," an annual training exercise much like REFORGER in Germany. I was teamed up with my Platoon Leader (a Captain) and a crew chief and given a Black Hawk to fly about the battlefield pretty much at will. We had a blast. We had to "sling load" (flying with pallets, fuel blivits, etc. under the helicopter attached by a sling to the cargo hook) various loads across the Team Spirit area. The first time I hovered in to hook up, I asked my co-pilot when he had last done a sling load. He said it had been over a year. I had not performed a sling load since my UH-60 qual. The crew chief had never done one. Pretty dumb and dangerous to continue, but we managed to successfully sling shit about the battlefield until Team Spirit was over.

We called Korea the "Land of Almost Right" due to the many things they would almost get right but not quite. There was a restaurant in Uijongbu that advertised "99 Kinds of German Beer and German Wurst" Several of us had been eyeing this place for some time and one day decided to give it a try. Sat down and ordered a German beer. Was told that they had only "OB," a Korean rot gut beer. What the hell? Asked about where the German beers were and was again told," We have only OB." So much for that. Ordered an

OB. Ordered some German wurst. What arrived were American hot-dogs with cheese. It was too ironic to even get pissed. Koreans tend to give you what they think you want instead of what you want. If you ask for a blue shirt and they have only green, they will try and convince you that you would look good in that green shirt. It's just the way it was.

A well-stocked fridge. Bud Light, OB, Soju (Korean liquor that would turn you into a "Soju warrior," capable of attempting just about anything stupid). Not sure what that jar of yellow shit was.

D Troop hosted a Thanksgiving dinner for a local orphanage in Uijongbu. The kids had a lot of fun. They really enjoyed the gambling machines in the NCO Club for some reason. The mess hall had prepared the usual Thanksgiving meal along with a Korean meal for our "KATUSAs" (Korean augmentation to the US Army, mostly rich Korean kids avoiding service in the Korean Army). Guess what the kids all ate? The Korean meal…kimchi (fermented cabbage), rice, and whatever type of meat the mess hall could come up with. Koreans eat rice and kimchi with every meal, so it was what they were comfortable with. Don't blame them. Spent my first Christmas away from home that year. Sucked. Returned to the States on 25 January 1988.

The three amigos, Van, I, and Jeff (note the distance sign on the right)

On to Ft. Campbell, Kentucky…

10.

1988 TO 1991 AT FT. CAMPBELL, KENTUCKY

Arrived at Ft. Campbell in March of 1988. I had applied for PTDY (permissive temporary duty) to attend the ERAU campus in Ft. Campbell and complete my associate degree. It was actually approved! Attended night classes in Ft. Campbell and completed my associate degree in mid-May.

I was then assigned to B Company 8th Battalion 101st Aviation Regiment. This was an AVIM (Aviation Intermediate Maintenance) Company. Initially, I was not particularly pleased with the assignment as I preferred to be performing at unit level, where the action was. Discovered AVIM life was just as challenging.

Attended the Air Assault Qualification Course in June of 1988. Figured I would just get it out of the way as it was supposedly required of all 101st soldiers. It was a challenging course, culminating with a 12-mile timed road march (especially dealing with the Kentucky June heat). Not a fan of rappelling (sliding down a rope from a helicopter). Graduated the course and pinned on the Air Assault badge. The badge was cool, a Huey helicopter imposed on wings.

The B Company CO called me into his office shortly after my assignment. I figured I had fucked something up and was expecting an ass-chewing. Instead, he assigned me to an accident investigation team. Would rather have had an ass-chewing. Accident investigations are incredibly detailed and intensive as their purpose is to find out why an accident occurred and recommend actions to prevent a similar event in the future. If a fatality is involved, it is even more detailed and intensive. This one turned out to be easy. A young LT had taxied a Black Hawk into an Exxon fuel sign. How does this happen, one might ask? In this case, the entire crew was at fault for not ensuring adequate rotor blade clearance. The rotor system cut through the beam holding the sign, the sign fell into the spinning rotor, the helicopter became extremely unbalanced as rotor blades and other parts of the rotor system left the aircraft, and the helicopter rolled over and was destroyed along with several small, fixed-wing aircraft damaged by flying debris. No fatalities, thank God. The LTs last name was Smutz. No shit. I will never forget his testimony, though. "LT Smutz, what happened?" "I taxied into a sign." Cut and dried, investigation complete. As a side note, there was a trailer nearby used to repair radios and such equipment. I was talking to the old guy that worked there. I was amazed that several components from the helicopter rotor system had punched through the wall of the trailer and destroyed several of the radios he was working on. Looked like a grenade had gone off inside. I asked how he had managed to avoid being struck by those parts. He replied that he had left to get a cup of coffee just prior to the accident. Lucky guy.

B 8-101st owned only three Huey helicopters. I made Huey PIC and began working on my Black Hawk PIC/MTP check rides. (Each time an aviator transfers to a new unit, he must complete check rides with the new unit IPs, a check and balance type of thing). I really enjoying flying the Huey again. I applied for the Huey MTP course and was accepted! Did not expect that. Headed to Ft. Eustis (AKA Ft. Useless) for the Huey MTP Course. The majority of the students were National Guard or Reserve since they owned most of the Huey fleet by then. I had a Major for my MTFE, a nice guy. He joked that I had more time at Ft. Eustis than he did. He said if I would fly along in the back for a few rides, he would get me finished when he was done with the guard and reserve guys (they were the priority). I was good with that. When my time came, he flew me for two flights and signed me off. Didn't hurt that I was already a Kiowa and Black Hawk MTP.

Ft. Rucker sent a team from DES to Ft. Campbell to conduct check rides on selected pilots. Being a new Huey PIC, I was selected. Again, lucky me. Also selected was our Battalion XO (Executive Officer), a Major who was also a new PIC. (Later went on to become a three-star General). He flew first and did well. I flew second. By then, the weather was turning to shit with low clouds and high winds. The DES IP decided he wanted to conduct an autorotation evaluation. Turned out the ceilings were too low for that. Thank God. He then decided he wanted to evaluate a maneuver called "Emergency Governor Operations" (The throttle is controlled manually). I advised against this as the winds were high and would make the maneuver extremely difficult. He insisted we continue. I totally fucked up the maneuver. Figured I was going to fail that check ride. He decided he would demonstrate how to correctly perform the maneuver. He totally fucked up the maneuver. Did I mention he was an Australian on temporary assignment to DES? Anyhow, after his poor execution of the maneuver, he said "It's too windy for this maneuver," with his Aussie accent. No shit Sherlock. I wanted to laugh but didn't in case there was a chance I would still pass the check ride. Passed the ride with flying colors. Go figure.

I had the pleasure of taking part in "The Great Pelican Caper." I, my flight school friend Butch, and my Korean roommate, Jeff, (they had also been assigned to Ft. Campbell), hatched a plan to kidnap a yard decoration belonging to Mark, one of Butch's friends. It was a large pelican. Why we decided this was a good idea, I'm not sure, but I am sure it involved a large quantity of alcohol. My wife and daughter were not innocent either, as they cut and pasted a ransom note from magazines. The ransom was a case of beer, delivered to Jeff's house at a designated time. We decided the heist would take place at night, so we came up with a plan. Jeff would haul Butch and me to a location near the target house in the back of his old Scout pick-up truck. After getting out of the Scout, we walked through a wooded area across the street from Mark's house. Butch and I ran across the road and went for the pelican. What we did not know was the pelican was cast out of concrete and weighed a ton. We managed to wrestle the pelican into an aviator's kit bag (a large canvas bag issued to pilots to carry gear in) and drug it back to our rendezvous location to meet Jeff. Back at Jeff's house, we took pictures of the now blindfolded pelican with a pistol pointed at its head, one with a sledgehammer about to crush the pelican's head, and another with an electric saw about to cut into it. (I'm guessing we took the film to the one-hour processing at Walgreens), and later dropped them, along with the ransom note, into Mark's mailbox. Mark arrived on time, on target, with the ransom in hand. We all had a great time. It was just silly fun.

Ransom note created by Pam and Kerry

(The *Pelican Brief* book was on the bestseller list at the time.)

Pelican hostage photo #1

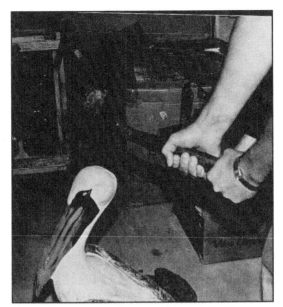

Pelican hostage photo #2

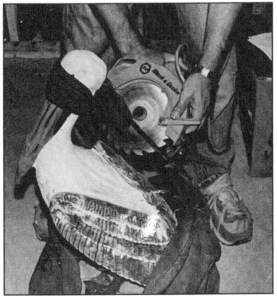

Pelican hostage photo #3

After the hostage release party

Made several training trips to Muskogee, Oklahoma. (We didn't smoke marijuana there either. Shout out to Merle Haggard). The airfield there was the staging point for missions into the "Box" (training area) at Ft. Smith, Arkansas. Mostly just a miserable existence for a couple of weeks.

I once again attempted an assessment for the 160th. This assessment was as demanding and brutal as the first time. Several flight academic tests are required, a PT test, Navy swim test, psychological written eval and interview with a shrink, and an aircraft NVG check ride. At the completion of this, you are subjected to an assessment board grilling—a stressful few days (to put it very mildly). The board consists of the president, usually the Regiment Commander or XO, the Regiment Psychologist, the IP that conducted the aircraft check ride, the Commander of the company you were assessing for, and the

Regiment Recruiting Officer. Each board member got a turn to fuck with you as much as they wanted. The IP I had flown with needed to leave, so the Board President had him give his flight debrief first. He said, "You got a U (unsatisfactory) for the flight; he's trainable," and left. I thought, *Well, hell.* Anyhow, I was approved by the board this time and had orders in my hand assigning me to the 160th in the fall of 1991. I was finally "IN."

Soto Cano Airbase, Honduras (4 months)

In the meantime, I was sent TDY (Temporary Duty) to Soto Cano Airbase, Honduras, to support JTFB (Joint Task Force Bravo) for four months. Soto Cano was divided in the middle by a 10,000-foot runway, with the Air Force and other services on one side and US Army pukes on the other. Our side was called Camp Blackjack. I think the only reason American forces are there is to occupy and protect that 10,000-foot runway. That runway would allow access for American forces to intervene, if necessary, in any Central American "issue."

We parked our Hueys on a ramp made of PSP (perforated steel planking). It was a cheap way to easily create a ramp, an idea left over from the Vietnam days. It worked but was mighty slippery. Any rapid throttle movements would spin the helicopter in its place (found that out quickly).

Hueys on the PSP ramp at Camp Blackjack

I was a Huey MTP as well as a Black Hawk MTP (We brought Black Hawks from the 101st down on C-5s). I was busy. We kept three of our seven old, beat-up Hueys in El Salvador to support the US Embassy there. They rotated one of them out about every week back to Soto Cano for maintenance. During a maintenance inspection, we found a bullet had penetrated the bulkhead of one of our Hueys behind the gunner's station. Normally the gunner is sitting there, so, must have had his head down, I guess. The bullet had gone through soundproofing around the bulkhead panel, had struck a fuel filter (luckily not penetrating it), and was lying on the transmission deck. No attacks were reported, so we figured it was just a random shot from some gorilla shithead. Our guys got lucky.

The mosquitoes were terrible. Slept with a mosquito net around my bunk. Had to. Was required to take Doxycycline every day to prevent malaria. First of many nasty third-world countries I deployed to with that requirement. Ate a lot of doxy over the years, but I never got malaria.

123

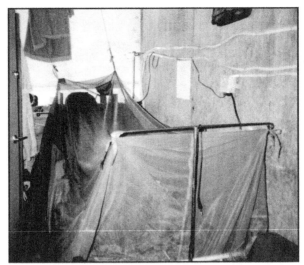

My bunk with mosquito net in Honduras

My "hootch" on Camp Blackjack

I agreed to fill in for the AMO (Aviation Maintenance Officer) while he went on leave (he was stationed there for a year, not part of our unit). As part of the perks, I was able to use his jeep to get back and forth around the airfield. Each morning I would have to go to the other side to update slides used to brief the JTFB Commander. Got a phone call one morning after the brief from some Captain chewing my ass about how I had misspelled Guatemala on the slide. (Well, hell, it must be some mental thing. I just spelled Guatemala wrong again but spellcheck fixed it. No spellcheck back then). We had sent three of our Black Hawks to Guatemala for a few days, and it was part of the slide to account for your aircraft. I said, "Ok, Sir, so I spelled Guatemala wrong. Did the Colonel happen to notice that three of my Hueys are "down" (as in broke)? He said no. Another case of leadership only concerned with appearances and not the genuine issues at hand. Also, he was an Infantry Colonel who did not know shit from apple butter about aviation or helicopters.

As I would drive around the airfield each morning, I would wave to a group of children that would always be outside the fence. I assumed that they were going to school until one day, I noticed that they were carrying machetes. The kids were going to work… most likely to harvest bananas or sugar cane. Sad, but not surprising, in a poor country like Honduras.

I became the owner of a "sea land container" (the large metal containers seen on the decks of cargo ships). It was packed with special tools used for maintenance of our UH-60 helicopters. I seldom went inside the container, as those tools were not often needed. Went in one day for something and was met by a huge red centipede with a thousand legs, which stood up on some of those legs and literally screamed at me. I'm not sure who was the most scared, but I got the hell out of that container and never went back. Who knew centipedes could scream?

There was an area near the runway that was fenced off and held several sea land containers. These were under constant guard by the Honduran Army and were referred to as the "Ollie vans" (Referencing LTC Ollie North, a supposed provider of weapons to the Nicaraguan rebels). Never found out what was in those containers, and probably wouldn't have wanted to know.

There was also an area that held several old, crashed Huey hulks. I often allowed the American Embassy flight personnel from the Honduran capital, Tegucigalpa, to raid parts from those hulks. Any aviation types will tell you that getting parts from a crashed helicopter was not good business, but what did I care? They weren't my helicopters. The Embassy Huey's had no tail numbers and basically "did not exist." I once flew down to Tegucigalpa in one of their Hueys to assist my engine mechanic with some engine maintenance that they did not have the required test equipment for (really just a reason to get us off of Camp Blackjack). Went on a test flight with their maintenance guy (a former Army MTP I knew from Ft. Lewis. Go figure). The tail number was actually written on the dash with a crayon. No shit. Ended up spending the night due to some excuse we made up. Had a good time and some tasty food and beer. I regularly traded beer with the Embassy guys for liquor (Liquor was not allowed on Soto Cano; the Embassy guys could not get American beer. Who the fuck knows why?) I would meet them on the ramp, and we would fill their helicopter with beer in exchange for liquor. A good trade for them and us.

A weekly highlight was a radio show called "Boss Talk" hosted by the JTFB Commander. Listeners would call in with problems that they thought needed fixing. It was hilarious. I never figured out if he was just going along with all the stupid shit that was called in or if he never really had a clue. Either way, it was mighty entertaining.

We grilled chicken nearly every night. Listened to Andrew "Dice" Clay nearly every night while grilling and drinking beer. It was funny every night. We were easily amused.

My guys decided they were going to catch an iguana. Why the hell that was, I don't know. Caught a skunk instead. Came to me for help. I backed off that one and said figure it out. Not sure how the skunk was released—probably by a team of Hondurans we called the "Mod Squad" for some reason. I called them when a huge swarm of bees landed and attached themselves to one of my maintenance hooch's. They informed me to just let them be, and they would move along in time. They did.

An iguana invaded the female shower hooch once, much to the amusement of everyone but the females in the shower at the time. Pretty funny. Don't remember how the invader was removed.

One of my soldiers was busted for failing a drug piss test. He swore he had not taken any drugs. I had to keep the kid locked up in a hooch until the test came back, confirming the substance that had made him test hot was not a drug but bee pollen. He was a weight-lifter and used bee pollen as a supplement. Who knew?

Spent my second Christmas deployed. Sucked again.

On New Year's Eve 1989, we had a huge party. Between the liquor I had traded for and what our guys from El Salvador had brought in, there was plenty of booze. I was really shit-faced, and at some point, I and one of my guys decided to moon the Blackjack Club. Proceeded to do so and was ejected from the club by a young LT that had drawn the short straw for SDO. Probably saved my career. Happened a lot, I guess—someone or something saving my career. I've been truly fortunate.

The JTFB Commander decided he would host an "officers call" on New Year's Day. Terrible idea. "Officers call" is when all the unit officers call on the commander in dress uniform. I was still badly hungover when I drove my loaned jeep to the other side of the runway to his headquarters building. The good thing was that so was everyone else, so it turned out ok. Day drinking day.

The Panama War kicked off in January of 1990. It did not affect us much, except the flow of parts that came from Panama was turned off for a couple of weeks.

When it was my time to leave Honduras, I sold my stuff (cooking utensils and whatnot I had bought from a departing soldier) to a Warrant Officer from the new unit from Panama that was taking over the Soto Cano rotation permanently. He would later be killed by rebels in El Salvador after his Huey was shot down. Good dude. That really sucked.

The CO for our group of guys and gals from Ft. Campbell was a single guy, so Pam agreed to be the acting commander's wife again. She did a great job, as always, dealing with whiny wives and the usual problems they had during deployments. It is true that as soon as you leave, everything on the home front goes to shit. If it can happen, it does. Always a challenge.

I returned to Ft. Campbell in February of 1990. Thought I was good to go for assignment to the 160th. After all, I had orders.

Saddam Hussain had different plans. In the fall of 1990, we were alerted to deploy to Saudi Arabia in support of Operation Desert Shield." My orders to the 160th were revoked. I was ok with that. Going to war was on my list of shit to do. Again, what a dumbass. Deployed to Saudi Arabia on 14 September.

Operation Desert Shield in Saudi Arabia

Initially, we were housed in the parking garage of King Fahd International Airport. It was stupid hot. I did get my own parking space.

My parking spot in the garage at King Fahd (about 100 degrees inside)

Mostly it was hours and hours of complete boredom. The battalion Sergeant Major had filled a shipping container with lawnmowers. Can you believe that? Guess he thought our soldiers would be busy mowing sand. Very typical of the leadership from our upper-level chain of command. Not focused on soldiers' training and welfare but on what the upper echelons would think of them.

One of my great memories was when we conducted a "camel recovery." A Cobra helicopter had crashed while attempting a landing in the desert and "browned out" or lost visual reference with the ground due to a dust cloud induced by the rotor system). Not at all unusual. The last 20 feet or so of a desert landing was usually a blind "Hold what you got" and hope you made it to ground ok. Sometimes when this happened, the crew would allow the helicopter to drift sideways or just land hard into the sand. This was the closest I have ever come to crashing. Picked a spot to land that we had landed in the day before, so we thought it would be ok. Did not know that a column of vehicles had passed through this spot the night before, turning the sand there into a foot of talcum powder. I let my co-pilot do the landing since he was better at "brownout" landings than I was. At some point, we realized this was not a usual brownout landing when we lost visual contact with the ground at about 50 feet. I allowed my co-pilot to continue since he had not communicated any issues, so I figured he was good to go. Not so much. We had begun drifting to the right, and the right landing wheel dug into the sand. At this point, the helicopter had nearly reached what we aviators call the point of no return, where the helicopter is going to roll over. I slapped the cyclic to the left as far as it would go. And the helicopter responded by rolling violently back to the left. I pulled a shit ton of collective, and we came out of the dust cloud like a rocket to the relief of all on board. I had about shit my pants—literally. Run-on landings then became my preference when at all possible. I did run-on landings (landing with forward movement) to some rough terrain where I probably should not have. After that when my Crew Chief started making the calls "Dust cloud at the tail." "Dust cloud at the cargo doors." "Dust cloud at the Gunner's door." "Dust cloud at your door." I would usually get the wheels on the ground by "dust cloud at your door" call regardless of the terrain or ground speed. Not smart, but to me, absolutely necessary.

"Dust cloud at the tail."

Back to the camel recovery. As we were going about lifting the Cobra helicopter onto a flatbed truck with a crane-type vehicle, a white hooptie (All the locals' vehicles there were white and called "hoopties." Don't ask.) appeared out of the desert. It was a Bedouin with a camel tied to the back of his hooptie. He approached us, and soon we figured out that he wanted us to use the crane to put the camel into the back of his hooptie. We figured, *What the hell*, and the Bedouin wrapped cargo straps around his camel, and we proceeded to pick up the camel (The Bedouin grabbed the camel by the lip to keep it from spinning.) and placed it in the back of his hooptie. He was a happy camper and drove off with a big smile. Building relationships with the locals, I reckon.

Crashed Cobra/camel recovery site.

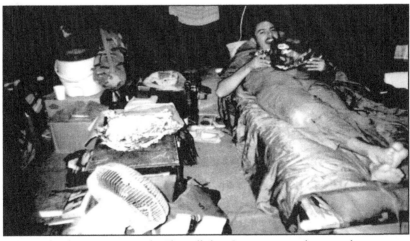

Thanksgiving in Saudi. Flew all day. Someone saved us a turkey.

Christmas in Saudi. Flew all day again. Someone saved us some turkey—again. This was my second Christmas in a row deployed. Sucked, again. Notice in the top left corner of the picture is a roll of Saddam Hussain shit paper someone sent me. I still have it.

Bob Hope came to King Fahd Airfield just before Christmas. Sat on top of a sealand container and tried to see the show. No luck. Did get to see his ride, an Air Force C-141 personalized for him.

Me in front of Bob Hope's C-141.

Me and my nephew Greg in Saudi. He was also assigned to the 101st. Judging from the soldier's silhouette in the background, I was preparing to haul some guys somewhere.

Desert Storm

The air war began on January 17th, 1991. There was no doubt when it seemed 1,000 Air Force sorties were launched from King Fahd that night. That also began the Scud missile attacks against Saudi and the US forces deployed there. During the first Scud attack, when the alarm went off, it was chaotic. Everyone was scrambling to get into a protective mask (gas mask) and get to a bunker. Patriot Missiles were deployed around King Fahd, and they began to launch to intercept the Scuds. There was a series of ear-shattering booms resulting in an "incoming" call. We had no idea the Patriots went supersonic and produced a sonic boom shortly after launch. That was the source of our booms. We realized later that no enemy rockets or mortars could reach us at King Fahd. Learned to sleep with a gas mask on. Not too hard, really. Learned to live with the fact that if a Scud hit our area, there wasn't shit you could do about it, so mostly ignored the Scud attacks. It either hits you, or it doesn't. And I know I said I never smoked again after quitting in 1977, but I figured, what the hell, if I'm going to get shot at, I'm going to smoke. I quit again as soon as we pulled out of Iraq.

Once watched an A-10 take off and lose a bomb from their bomb rack. It bounced down the runway with us expecting it to explode. It didn't. A pickup loaded with Air Force dudes came out and loaded the bomb into the back of the truck. I assume the A-10 completed the mission just short a bomb. The A-10s would regularly return from missions shot to hell. They would land with no hydraulics, and large chunks shot out of their wings. Huge kudos to those guys; and gals; they were taking it to the Iraqis bigtime.

One day, my buddy Chuck and I were standing near the flight line when we heard what sounded like a rocket being launched from one of the Apache helicopters parked on the ramp. We both said that at least it missed the Chinook helicopters parked in front of it (how stupid was that? You never park armed aircraft behind anything), and there wasn't anything across the runway but an ammo dump, and how unlikely it was that it would hit it. About that time, a huge explosion occurred, followed by a large mushroom cloud appearing from where the ammo dump was. Turns out the Apache had accidentally launched a Hellfire missile that just happened to hit the dump. My friend Eric was on an approach for landing in a Huey when the dump blew up. Scared the shit out of him and his crew. Shit like that happens occasionally; guys get careless with switches and procedures.

Once during an in-ranks inspection; I know how stupid that sounds, but this happened. Anyhow, we were being inspected by the Battalion CO and the Sergeant Major (same Sergeant Major that brought the lawnmowers) for such infractions as needing a haircut or mustache trim. A Scud attack began with the sirens and alarms. The CO and Sergeant Major continued the inspection until we all broke ranks and scattered like roaches for the bunkers. The CO and Sergeant Major were left standing alone in a field of dust, looking like fools.

My company CO proved what a fool he was a couple of weeks after the war had started when he decided we needed a training exercise outside the confines of the airfield. This was called an ARTEP (Army Training and Evaluation Program). It was to check the block so their report cards would look good. I asked our CO if someone had coordinated with the MP checkpoint leading into the airfield, as we would be conducting simulated attacks using blank ammunition near their checkpoint. The MPs had real ammo as they should have. Turns out no one had talked to them. I stated that was just foolish, and it went downhill from there. Still convinced that was why all officers in the battalion were awarded a Bronze Star after the war, but me and my buddy Chuck, another Warrant Officer not afraid to tell it like it was. I'm good with that. It was worth it.

We forward deployed around the end of January to an area about ten miles west of the Iraqi border. This would be our kick-off point when the ground war started. (We all knew a ground war was inevitable and, by this point, just wanted to get on with it.)

I was flying along Tap Line Road, a route between the Kuwait border and Saudi. Noticed that the ground convoy under us was in full MOPP (Mission Orientated Protective Posture) 4 or wearing a full set of chemical and nuclear attack protective gear. Decided to land in case I had missed such an attack or impending attack. Sent my Crew Chief out to figure out what was happening. In the meantime, another convoy approached us wearing T-shirts and shorts. Decided this was total bullshit and continued to our destination.

Another time I was flying into KKMC (King Khalid Military City Airfield) when I began to fly over what appeared to be an entire Armored Division on the move. Never before or since have I seen such a display of pure military power. Impressive. Figured I had not gotten the memo regarding the invasion of Iraq and the start of the ground war and was just dumbly flying across a division boundary. Turns out it was a false alarm, and the Division was halted at the border. Sucked for them but was fortunate for us as we became "air pirates," raiding their abandoned camps and acquiring much-needed equipment they had left in their haste to get to the battle. I slingloaded an intact wooden shower back to our camp. We were quite the heroes.

Some nutcase decided we should conduct "stand to," something left over from wars long before this one. Had done this as a Tanker during REFORGER in Germany. It involved getting up before 6 am to man stations for battle. Totally worthless. Froze our asses off. Served no purpose other than to irritate all of us. It did. We adopted the Garth Brooks song "Friends in Low Places" as our stand-to song.

On stand to in Saudi. So damn stupid! NVGs in case at bottom right so we
could see the sneaky bastards before daylight—just plain stupid.

I asked for a gunnery range to train our door gunners for shooting from a flying helicopter. Not something we had trained for. How
dumb was that? Was told, "You don't need that, and it's too hard to
coordinate." What a crock of shit! I decided to conduct my own range.
There were many abandoned hoopties in the middle of the desert—perfect targets for my guys to train on. So, on each flight, I would allow
my guys to engage those hoopties. My guys were well-trained by the
time the invasion of Iraq was upon us. Not sure how we accounted for
the expended ammo; I left that to my door gunners, who worked it out
somehow. They did not want to invade Iraq not trained in gunnery.

On 24 February, the ground war invasion of Iraq started, and on 25 February, my crew and I made our first flight into Iraq. The 101st had set up a base in the desert about 100 miles inside Iraq. It was occupied by all of the 101st elements, so as you can imagine, it was a large area spread out over the desert. We bounced around that area for a while, trying to find the B Company element that had deployed the day before. It was pretty much a goatfuck. Finally found them. The next day, a shamal rolled in, so the war stopped for a day. The sandstorms, or "shamals" as they were called, were usually a 24-hour period of high winds and zero visibility. Everything inside the helicopter would become covered with about a half inch of sand. What wasn't tied down or attached to something was blown away. No flight or ground operations could be conducted. We stayed inside the helicopter until it passed.

I learned that helicopter emergency procedures are not all cut and dried; some required thought, and some needed to be ignored. Case in point, about halfway between our Saudi camp and our Iraqi camp, a fuel filter light illuminated on my caution panel. I executed the emergency procedure by the book, backed up with the checklist. The emergency procedure required that the fuel lever on the engine with the filter light be moved to "cross feed," where both engines ran off the opposite tank of fuel. Quickly figured out that with both engines running off the same fuel tank, I would run out of fuel long before reaching our camp in Iraq. Returned that engine's fuel lever to feed from the normal tank and hoped for the best. One running engine is always better than no engines running because you followed the emergency procedure to the letter. Made it back to camp with no issues. Lesson learned: back up the checklist with common sense.

The prisoner-of-war camps was amusing for us. When we would fly over them, the prisoners would run to the opposite side of the camp, so when we flew around them it was much like herding sheep. Fun for us, who were extremely bored with this war.

I made the promotion list for CW3 while living in the parking garage at King Fahd. I was reminded of the Bill Murray character in *Stripes* when he said, "That means so much to a man who cleans garbage cans for a living." I was probably insubordinate to the Battalion CO, who appeared in front of my parking space with the good news as I was wallowing in about an inch of sweat on top of my sleeping bag. Pretty much said thanks and who gives a fuck? Not good. It takes a while to receive orders making this official. I still had not received them when we deployed to Iraq. I asked my friend Eric, a Lieutenant, to make sure he intercepted my orders and flew to our camp in Iraq to promote me since I did not want to be promoted by the clown shoes CO I served under. He was good to his word and arrived in our camp by Huey one day with my promotion orders in hand, tore off my CW2 nametag (attached with Velcro), replaced it with my CW3 nametag, we exchanged salutes, and he returned to the camp in Saudi. A few weeks later, my CO conducted a three Huey Air Assault mission into our camp in Iraq. He brought a copy of my orders, intending to promote me. When he discovered I had already been promoted, he was not a happy camper. But I'm sure he found solace in awarding all the participants in his flight air medals for their heroic assault into enemy territory. Pure bullshit.

Promotion to CW3 in Iraq (note trusty .38 caliber pistol. I carried a snack bag with 18 bullets in it besides the 6 in the cylinder. I felt like Barney Fife).

We lived in our Black Hawk while in Iraq. When it got dark, we went to bed. When it became light, we would get up. Listened to the soundtrack from *Good Morning Vietnam* every night. It was funny every night. Discovered a million different ways to prepare an MRE (meal ready to eat).

THE UNOFFICIAL MRE* RECIPE BOOKLET

HOW TO HAVE FUN EATIN' ON THE RUN

Mort Walker

*(Meals, Ready-to-Excite)   © King Features Syndicate, Inc.

DESERT STORM EDITION:
THE OFFICIAL UPDATE OF THE
UNOFFICIAL MRE COOKBOOK

(Now your rations can be Meals Relished by Eaters)

SCUD BUSTER STEW

Obviously, someone SCUD-ed a chicken to make the stew in Menu 03. Sweet 'n sour it up with a little hot pepper heat to give it personality.

    1   pouch chicken stew (Menu 03)
    1/2 pouch peaches reconstituted
    1   spoonful (small) lemon-lime drink mix, dry
    TABASCO® pepper sauce to taste (at least 3 dashes)

Add peaches, dry lemon-lime drink mix and several dashes of TABASCO® pepper sauce to warmed chicken stew. Give it a good stir and be surprised!

STEALTH BOMBER TUNA

Sneak up on tuna with noodles and spice it up when it's not looking. A little cheese, a few olives and a generous splash of TABASCO® will do it.

    1   pouch tuna with noodles (Menu 10)
    1   pouch cheese spread (Menu 10)
    8-10 pitted green or ripe olives, sliced
    4   generous dashes TABASCO® pepper sauce

Add cheese spread, sliced olives and TABASCO® pepper sauce to warmed tuna with noodles. Mix well and rejoice.

AT EASE OMELET

This is an at-easy one: open up warmed potatoes au gratin from the ham omelet meal (Menu 04), add about a half-teaspoon of mustard and two dashes of TABASCO® pepper sauce. Pour it over the warmed omelet. Outstanding!

Note that Tabasco sauce is added to each recipe. A tiny bottle came in all MREs. Used by GIs to kill the taste of just about everything.

Home sweet home for about a hundred days.

Laundry day in Iraq. Hopefully, there would be no "no-notice" flights.

The sand took a terrible toll on the Division's helicopter engines and rotor systems. I became a traveling "jump start" for helicopters that had APUs (auxiliary power units) that would not start. When I got a call, I would find the broken helicopter's location on the map and decide if I had the fuel necessary to get there and back while slinging an AGPU (Aircraft Ground Power Unit). If I did, we would pick up the AGPU and depart. Upon arrival at the site, I would set the AGPU down, punch off the sling, and land. My guys would move the AGPU to the broken helicopter (the AGPU had its own power to move on land). We would then perform what was called a "blow start," using the air and electrical power from the AGPU to start the helicopter. Once the helicopter was started, we would reverse the procedure and be about the battlefield to the next broken helicopter location. A flying service station. Worked pretty well.

Flew the DISCOM (Division Support Command) Commander to Basra. Asked him where he wanted to go, and he said just look for a bunch of antennas and land. Turned out he was right, and we got him where he needed to be. He was really a great guy but did not like to fly. Whenever we landed, he would be out of the helicopter as soon as it touched down to light up a cigarette with his minions in tow. A full bird colonel usually has a couple of captains with him as "assistants." On this same flight, we passed over a broken-down flat-bed trailer left behind on the road in the middle of the desert, loaded with pallets of MREs. On the flight back, when we passed by, it was empty. Guess the Bedouins were not too picky about what they ate. Lots of pork meals in those too. Makes you wonder.

Watched many flights of B-52s inbound to bomb Iraq. Glad I was not on the receiving end of that. They always had fighter escorts. Watched the fighters return from hitting targets and join up with KC-135 Tankers and perform air-to-air refueling. Pretty interesting stuff.

Flew over a site where the much-feared Republican Guard Tank Unit had battled it out with US ground forces. They lost. Very few turrets were still on their tanks. Every tank had been shot many times. Made me wish I had been a tanker again—that had to be a rush.

The war lasted about three days. Personally, I wished we had finished off Saddam while we were there (would have saved the second Iraq invasion). Stayed in Iraq for about another month. We returned to King Fahd, cleaned and serviced our equipment as best we could, and caught a flight back to Ft. Campbell in April.

Back at Ft. Campbell with Pam and Kerry.

Even my commode missed me.

We washed our uniforms and flight suits in plastic tubs. Thought we were getting them clean. When I did a load of them back home, the bottom of the washer had a coat of mud in it. So much for thinking we were getting them clean.

Spent about a month in Jacksonville, Florida, recovering our Black Hawks off the container ships they were shipped back from Iraq in. There was a huge parking lot filled with new cars that had been off-loaded from Japan and other countries. All had keys in them, so had quite a time joy riding around in them, and nobody seemed to care. When the mission was completed, found out that the 101st had stopped running the buses used to ferry crews back and forth to Jacksonville. When I asked how we were supposed to get home, the answer was: however you can. So, I went looking for a ride home for us. Finally wound up in a Navy Air Guard Unit that operated the P-3 Orion (a fixed-wing submarine hunter). They had a flight headed to New Orleans, but I figured that would get us closer to Ft. Campbell, at least. When we were in the air, I was able to talk to the pilots, one of whom happened to be a former Cobra helicopter pilot from the Vietnam War. When he heard of our dilemma, he rerouted his flight to stop at Campbell Army Airfield and drop us off. The Campbell Airfield guys could not figure out why a P-3 had landed there. They did not have a set of steps that was compatible with the P-3, so we ended up climbing out on a forklift with a pallet on it. Did not mind at all. The pilot gave the Campbell ATC (air traffic control) folks a ration of shit about abandoning their soldiers in Jacksonville and having to be rescued by the Navy. What a great guy to do that for us.

Back at Ft. Campbell

It was business as usual back at Ft. Campbell. One of the captains I worked with in 8th Battalion had been assigned to the 6th Battalion upon return to Ft. Campbell. One of their Hueys developed a problem with its fuel system with clogged fuel filters. They finally decided to open the fuel cell to investigate what was causing the clogs. When they opened the cell, they found a hand grenade inside, taped with "100 MPH Tape" or military-grade duct tape. To quote the Captain (a Black guy), "I turned white and about shit my pants." They called the EOD (Explosive Ordinance Disposal) Unit who disposed of the grenade. Figured it had been placed inside the fuel cell before the aircraft was loaded into the ship in Saudi. Would have been catastrophic had the grenade exploded inside the ship.

Good thing 100 MPH Tape is strong. They never figured out how or why the grenade ended up in the fuel cell.

Talked to DA. They would not release me to the 160th, saying that the 160th had plenty of Black Hawk MTPs. Told me to expect another tour of Korea. Great. Got a call one day from a Major that was the F Company CO with 1/160th. Wanted to interview me. The interview went well; he needed "Little Bird" (a variant of the OH-6 Cayuse helicopter) MTPs as well as Black Hawk MTPs. With my OH-58 and Black Hawk experience, he thought I would fit in well with his maintenance company, which worked on both Little Birds and Black Hawks. I told him about DA's reluctance to release me to the 160th. He said he would have my orders in three days. Right. Went back to work, not really expecting anything to change. Three days later, orders arrived in the mail assigning me to the 160th. That Major had serious contacts in Washington.

Also, in August of 1991, I completed my bachelor's degree with Embry Riddle. Really wanted to get that finished prior to my 160th assignment, as I knew I would have little time for anything outside of the unit. Little did I know.

On to the 160th...

11.

1991 TO 1998 AT F 1/160TH SOAR

F 1/160 is known as the "Dominators."

I was assigned to F Company 1/160th SOAR (Special Operations Aviation Regiment) in the fall of 1991. Every soldier must complete "Green Platoon" training. Green Platoon trains 160th soldiers in basic skills such as land navigation, weapons training, Combat Medical Training, Close Quarters Combat, and of course, a large amount of PT. I did not have a Green Platoon class scheduled until February, so the F Company CO requested that I be allowed to begin training as a Little Bird Pilot and MTP. This was a highly unusual request since soldiers in Green Platoon are normally segregated from unit operations and personnel until completion of Green Platoon. The Battalion Commander was very reluctant to approve the request but did so after much convincing by the F company CO. So, I began the AQC for the MH-6C Cayuse helicopter. I completed the AQC with no issues; I really enjoyed flying that helicopter. It was very maneuverable and just fun to fly. After the MH6C AQC, I moved on to the AH/MH-6J AQC. This, too, proved to be a lot of fun. Another very maneuverable helicopter, even more than the MH6C, with more power. I was trained to land on buildings and in extremely small areas. I was having a blast. I went on to the MTP part of the M/AH-6 training with a great guy named Brady, who taught me well how to perform test flights and track and balance the main rotor of that helicopter. I was in a pure state of helicopter heaven as I was allowed to do nothing but train with Brady. It was such a change from the usual training environment of being in a structured classroom and flight line. I learned at a rapid pace in a great teaching environment from a great MTFE. I passed my MTP check ride and was performing MTFs in the unit when I had a "hot start" issue. I was starting an MH-6 for a routine run-up. When I pressed the start button for engine start, the engine immediately ignited, and the temperature spiked and exceeded limitations, as in I melted the engine. I checked the throttle to ensure it was off and found that I had pressed the start button with the throttle at idle. Bad shit. Got it shut down, reported it to maintenance, and documented what had happened in the aircraft logbook. Expected the worst, and found nobody was really concerned about it, and they went about replacing the engine. In a regular unit, I would have been required to make a formal report to the Unit Safety Officer who would have been required to report it to Mother Rucker, who would classify it as a Class B or C accident based on the cost to repair/replace the engine, and I would have been subjected to additional training and check rides to ensure I was trained and proficient or not. Later, the Battalion Commander was concerned that I might need additional training and was not ready to be a Little Bird MTP. Turns out the Battalion Commander torched an engine himself the next day, so my problems went away.

Attended the dreaded SERE (Survival, Evasion, Resistance and Escape) Level C (Level C includes what is called a "Resistance Laboratory" or prisoner camp) school at North Island NAS (Naval Air Station), San Diego, California, 7 through 16 January 1992. I figured hey, San Diego in January can't be too bad, right? Wrong. The academics were in San Diego, but the hands-on training was in the mountains near San Diego, around 3,000 feet. Went through a few days of academics and then was bused to the mountain training site. SERE school is designed to train one to survive as a POW (prisoner of war). The other steps of survival and evasion are taught, but the essence of the training is how to resist and escape if a POW. We were sent out in small teams to navigate and evade capture. There were administrative moments along the way. One evening, we were together with a large group to kill and eat a couple of rabbits. I have not mentioned that this was a Navy SERE Course, so the students were mostly young Navy aviators and crew members, a few Marines, and a couple of Navy Seals. They really did not know what an Army Warrant Officer was. When the time came to kill the rabbits, they asked for volunteers, and only me and my friend Eddy (another F Company Little Bird MTP) were up to the deed. We were both country boys, and we were hungry. I think about half of the group nearly fainted when we killed those rabbits, but they sure weren't afraid to eat them. We boiled them in a big pot with some added rice, and it amounted to about a cup per student that tasted like the rabbit had waded through the water with boots on. I was in a group of five guys, and again, I did all the navigating. I guess Navy types don't get much training using a map.

I ended up snuggling with a young Navy LT one night; it was just stupid cold. It was so cold one night they called an administrative break to build a fire. Guessing it was around 10 degrees. My group had avoided getting captured (which meant less time in the "Camp"), so they blew a horn which meant the end of this part of the training. They placed hoods over our heads and loaded us up for transport to the "POW" camp. Much of what goes on in these "Camps" is better left to your imagination. We were beaten regularly (without breaking any bones), subjected to numerous interrogations, placed into extremely small boxes, and humiliated in various ways. You haven't lived until you've done pushups and jumping jacks naked in 10-degree weather. I should mention that during all this, we were allowed no sleep, and I can tell you that sleep deprivation is much worse than hunger. There was an almost constant broadcasting of propaganda in some foreign language, and at some point, I began to hear it in English. I was being taken out of my box and thumped on a regular basis and was wondering why; then I realized my box was under a flood light, and they wanted to make sure all the other prisoners could see a prisoner getting thumped. Lucky me. The resistance part ended in a couple of days—a couple of long days and longer nights. At my debrief, I was told I had made most of the mistakes all students make. I told the guy that had repeatedly thumped my ass that he was, well, well-trained. I had never and still have never had such a unique training experience. You will never feel the same when you see the American and POW/MIA flags after this experience. You get it. It should be noted that I was 36 years old when I attended SERE. I was known in the camp as "The Ancient One." Shows how young the other students were.

Finally started Green Platoon on 3 February. Green Platoon was fun minus the PT. They PTed the dog shit out of us. The weapons ranges were particularly fun. We shot a shit ton of ammo while running, standing, crouching, and doing anything you could think of while shooting a weapon. At the time, the unit had MP-5 machine guns—9 mm weapons that were a pleasure to shoot. Really fun, accurate guns. Had a course in close combat hand-to-hand skills. I was not particularly good at this. I was unfortunate enough to be teamed with an ex-Special Forces guy for this training, who proceeded to beat the shit out of me at every opportunity. I tried to convince him that this was just a training event, but he did not get it. I was so black and blue that by the end of the course, I looked like a gang of thugs had beaten me. A gang of one, as it turned out. Still managed to gain skills I would never have gotten otherwise. The land navigation course was not that challenging, but I was wondering about the small signs marking the targets with the letters NSDQ on them. Finally, asked someone what that stood for and was told, "Night Stalkers don't quit." It is the unit's motto. Learned to live by it. We also guarantee to be on target "+ or - 30 seconds" anywhere in the world. The 160th has never been on target outside of that + or – 30-second window…ever.

Took a bus along with other Green Platoon Officers to Jacksonville, Florida, 27 thru 29 February for my first of many Dunker quals (qualifications). Quite an experience. Being strapped into a large barrel with a bunch of other guys and sank under water, then rolled inverted, then finding your way to the surface was damn exciting as in scary as hell. Did this in the dark also from several positions in the barrel (simulating a helicopter cabin). Great training when it's over, as usual. Finished Green Platoon on Friday, 13 March.

Dunker training sucked but was still great training.

Jumped on the 160th train the following Monday, and that train never slowed down for the next seven years. I will break the next seven years down by deployments—easier than keeping up with time at home, which wasn't much. I know this is mostly boring routine deployment shit, but I can't figure out another way to depict the constant training and deployment environment in the 160th. It was fun but very demanding on my family and me. Was issued a beeper (dating myself, I know) and was on call for the majority of the next seven years.

The method of transportation for these deployments was one of three ways: self-deploy via helicopter, load onto Air Force transport planes (C-141, C-130, or C-5), or commercial air. Occasionally, we would get a rental car and drive if the situation deemed it practical. The C-5 is a massive aircraft that allowed us to pack an entire "Bullet" (go-to-war package) on one aircraft. It was quite an experience to see helicopters and a shit ton of equipment get loaded up. There would literally be only inches or less between pieces of equipment.

Deployed on my first mission with the 160th on 16 March through 29 March to a classified location in Nevada two days after completing Green Platoon. Had a blast as, again, I was left alone to do something I was really good at, troubleshooting and test-flying helicopters. Upon return to Ft. Campbell, finally asked if I was allowed to wear the coveted red beret members of the unit proudly wore. I never attended the Green Platoon graduation ceremony (I think I was test flying), where the berets are presented to all graduates, so, had to ask. Someone said, "Sure."

6-10 April deployed to Pope Air Force Base/Ft Bragg, North Carolina. This was the first of many CAPEX (Capabilities Exercise) missions I would deploy on. These were "dog and pony show" put on for politicians from DC to see how the taxpayer money was being spent, as well as to garner more money for the Special Operations community. It was mostly fun, especially my first one since I had not seen our "customers" in action. (Delta Force, Seal Team 6, and Army Rangers—I know, supposed to be classified but more information can be found on YouTube and Google now than I knew then). For one demo, the Seal Team Commander would stand next to a window of a shoot house (a building used for live fire training) with a balloon floating in the window with a face painted on it. One of the Team's snipers would take a live shot and shoot the balloon—always good for a thrill for the politicians (and more money). The MH guys would conduct an assault on the shoot house, and the customers would shoot the shit out of the place. Our Little Bird gunships and DAP (Defensive Armed Penetrator) Black Hawks would always put on quite a show at the range also. Mo' money.

Attended Little Bird School (MD Helicopter) in Phoenix, Arizona, 26 April thru 8 May. Another great school. Learned how civilians maintained their version of the Little Bird. We sent all our Little Bird MTPs to this school as well as our TIs (Technical Inspectors) and other MOSs when able.

Deployed to Ft. Benning, Georgia, in May, but not sure of the dates or what type of trip it was. Most likely an FTX (Field Training Exercise, joint training with all the players). Completed RL1 and NVG PIC in an A/MH6 series during this trip.

Completed MH60L AQC and MH60 MTP course in July. I was now currently flying MH6C, A/MH6G/H/J, and MH60A/L helicopters. It was a busy time, but I was living the dream.

Attended the Allison Engine School in Indianapolis, Indiana, 20 thru 24 July. Highlight of this school was getting shitfaced and singing karaoke in the hotel bar. And to repeat—another great school.

Deployed to Ft Bragg, North Carolina, 2 thru 8 August. Got my first flight to land on a pitched rooftop with guys on the pods. I would not have jumped onto that roof under any condition, but those guys made it seem easy. Also got to fast-rope customers onto an elevated platform (a tall building). Guys slide down thick ropes attached to the helicopter; when they are on the target, the ropes are released.

Little Bird "Fast Roping" customers onto a building

Deployed to Ft. Bragg, North Carolina, 24 and 25 September for a 2-day trip to repair and test fly a broken Little Bird at that location. Happened quite often. If it were a small number of aircraft, we would not send an MTP on the trip and would deploy as necessary to fix the broken helicopter.

Deployed to Savannah, Georgia, 13 thru 17 October. Another trip to fix a broken bird. Savannah is a nice place to deploy to usually, but not if you end up living in "Sabre Hall," a barracks located on Hunter Army Airfield. Rooms were ok but had the usual shared latrines and showers.

Completed the A/MH6 NOTAR (No Tail Rotor) AQC in October. The Unit had modified two of our Little Birds into NOTAR configurations for testing to see if the NOTAR would work for us. Turned out it did not. Handling and power issues shut down that test.

157

AH-6 NOTAR on the right.

Coca, Ecuador

Deployed on 4 November to Panama to fill in as an MH60 MTP
for the 617th SOAD (Special Operations Aviation Detachment), a
160th asset stationed at Howard Airforce Base in Panama. Deployed
from Howard to Coca, Ecuador, on 11 November. This would be a
really fun deployment. I had never been in a jungle environment before. Things in the jungle are different. Coca is a small village located
in the Amazon rainforest at the confluence of the Coca and Napo
rivers. We stayed in the only hotel in the Ville which catered to us
Yankees. The food was great; the beer was cheap. I ordered the same
thing for breakfast every morning and got something different almost
every day. Same for lunch and dinner. I'm sure my lame attempts at
speaking Spanish did not help. If juice were ordered, they would
literally go out back, pick it off a tree, and put it in a blender. Tasty.

Most of the insects there were large. Scary large. And ugly. The Ville was powered by a generator which normally was shut down around 10 pm each night. While we were there, we would send money to the generator guy to keep it running later for our nightly shenanigans, so the Coca people loved it when we were in town. One night, while in the middle of a poker game, my friend Larry had a large ugly insect of some kind flap up and land on his shoulder. I would have shit, but Larry calmly asked the ugly fucker, "Should I raise or fold?" We all lost it. Very funny moment. A meal in the Ville cost about three bucks and was generally very tasty and filling. Returning to the hotel one night, we came upon a guy with a Caiman (small alligator of some kind). He was chopping at the caiman's head with a dull, rusty machete. He asked if the Yankees would like to help kill the caiman, so we each took a turn with the machete. He invited us back the next day to help eat the caiman fried in what I'm sure was 10-year-old grease. Turned out that was some really good meat. Twice while we were there, I saw two pygmies (Yes, there were real pygmies) carrying a large (about 150 pounds of large) catfish through the street. They had a 2x4 piece of wood through the gills to facilitate carrying the catfish. The Ville feasted on catfish for about a week. The jungle also was populated with women with those long choking things around their necks to make their necks seem about three feet long. Dishpan-sized earrings. Large pans in their lips. Thought this was shit that only existed in National Geographic.

We were deployed to perform drug interdiction along with a team of SF guys and two DEA agents. We worked with the Ecuadorian Army as well. The locals were not interested in enforcing any drug interdiction due to the threat from the cartels to kill them, their families, and anyone connected to them. Flying there was challenging. When it rained there, it fucking rained as in zero forward visibility. Visibility to the side was probably about a mile but forward was zero. Fortunately, we had flown most routes before and knew there was nothing above tree level anywhere, so it was ok to just cruise along until we got out of the rain. We would be flying over the triple canopy jungle most of the time for miles with nothing to be seen below when, out of nowhere, an airfield would appear. Wonder what that was for? Only one reason for an airfield in the middle of the jungle. Mark it on the map and continue the mission. Stopped by an Air Force radar sight at an airfield somewhere north of Coca. They were tracking aircraft flights all over the Amazon Valley section of Ecuador with black markers on a large map. It looked like a kid had randomly drawn lines all over the map. I asked what they did with the data and was told: nothing. Once during a stop there, the locals started to shoot at us, or at least a few rounds came our way. Don't really think they were intentionally shooting at us; they were rioting at the time over some oil tax money that provided a few cents a week to the citizens and had been discontinued by the oil companies. Anyhow, my guys and I locked and loaded, and we dashed off the site headed to our Black Hawk. The plan was to make a quick start and get the fuck out of there. I had previously had problems getting the starter to engage on this Black Hawk, so I ended up doing what we called a pencil start where a pencil is inserted into the start controls onto a microswitch to force engagement of the starter. So, instead of making a grand escape, we looked like a Three Stooges act. Departed the area without further incident. I ended up taping a pencil to the dash of that aircraft kind of as a joke, but ready to admit, neither my guys nor I were ever able to figure out what the fuck was wrong with the start system. It was a daily event to watch the GPS countdown to all zeros at the Equator and then start counting up again. It was like flying in Death Valley and watching the altimeter (altitude indicator) indicate negative altitude. Only a few places on Earth where shit like that happens.

There was an Ecuadorian Army post near the border with Peru. We went there regularly and so kept a couple of blivits of fuel available, which required that we leave one of our fuel handlers to stay at the camp. The Ecuadorian Army had camp whores. Just a fact. She would service, I guess, a few (few being a number that only leaves you guessing) guys each night. Our fuel guy got on the list when he arrived and was number 101. His number came up before we returned him and our blivits to Coca (I realize the few guys a day math does not work out. I don't know, maybe our guy was allowed to move up the line since he was leaving) for redeployment to Panama, so he was a happy camper. When I left Coca, I caught a ride with our money guy, Angel. Angel carried a briefcase full of Ecuadorian money to cover those unexpected expenses. One of our guys crashed a rent Angel bought a new one. You know, that kind of thing. Angel was an Army SFC, but really was our liaison with the locals since he spoke fluent Spanish and had a vast knowledge of the local customs and whatnot. We drove a Land Rover from Coca to Quito, Ecuador. Sea level to 10,000 feet, through the Andes Mountains in a Land Rover. Crossed bridges that shouldn't have been crossed (they looked like something out of Indiana Jones) and avoided "cowboys,"— armed locals (robbers). Angel was armed but only with a 9MM pistol, and I was unarmed, not a good plan. Made it to Quito ok. Quite an experience. Quito is an exceptionally beautiful European type of city with the Equator running right through the middle (hence Ecuador). I recently googled Coca, and, wow, that place has grown. Several hotels and a population of 46,000 plus. (It has been about 30 years as of this writing). Returned to Ft. Campbell 10 December. Not one damn picture from this deployment. End of 1992.

Back to Ft. Campbell...

Attended an MTP Conference in Williamsburg, Virginia 24-29 January 1993. This was a get-together of MTPs from across the Army to attend classes and briefings related to maintenance and Maintenance Test Flights (Actually an excuse to party with other MTPs). Had my buddy Angel (not the Angel from Panama) beep my beeper to fake urgent calls and got out of some of the most boring briefings.

Deployed on what we call an "Under Way" from 20 February to 26 February. This was my first experience aboard a Navy ship, the USS Belleau Wood. We deployed from Okinawa, Japan, out to the ship. I rode out aboard a Little Bird on the plank (an attachment to the side of our MH Little Birds to transport passengers). As we approached the ship, I noticed that there was a trail of trash from the stern of the ship and asked what was with that. Found out it was trash time, which happens about three times a day when all trash is dumped into the ocean. So much for EPA (Environmental Protection Agency) rules at sea. My bag with all my clothes and such was left on shore due to a flight being overloaded, so I had no clean clothes with me. Luckily, one of the Little Bird pilots was about my size and loaned me a flight suit and a few clean pairs of underwear. Aboard a Navy ship, I encountered the most prejudiced rank environment I have worked in. The Navy has their ship divided into countries as in Officer's Country, Chief's Country, and lower enlisted scum country. One does not venture into the Chief's Country, and vice versa; Chiefs do not venture into Officer's Country. Took me forever to figure out how to get about the ship divided by levels and passageways closed for about anything, requiring an alternative route to get to say, the Officer's Mess. (Yes, they have separate dining areas for Officers, Chiefs, and Enlisted. I snuck my TI into the Officer's Mess and received an ass-chewing from my Battalion CO. You just don't do that shit. Unreal.) When the ship's captain declared the "Smoking lamp lit," I swear the stern (back) of the boat would sink a few feet due to a large number of smokers rushing to the stern to smoke (the only smoking-allowed location on the boat). Mostly a miserable trip lightened only by one of the SOCOM (Special Operations Command) Commander's comments about our helicopters launching on a night "as black as my ex-wife's heart."

The Sea of Japan where we were operating was very rough. Several times I had to strap myself in my bunk to sleep to avoid getting thrown out from the rough seas. This was also my first experience with the "blue bombers," pills taken to knock you out for about ten hours and leave you refreshed and ready for the mission upon arrival at the mission site. Those damn things were great. As a note, this trip required a certain level of training and proven competence and testing to be the OIC (Officer in Charge) for a deployment OCONUS (Out of the Contiguous United States). It was a designation for an FMQ (Fully Mission Qualified) MTP. I was not, until the F Company IPs/FMQs figured out this was a shit trip, and guess what? I was instantly designated an FMQ. Go figure. Returned to Ft. Campbell 26 February.

13-26 April deployed to Muskogee, Oklahoma, to play games in the box again much as I had with the 101st. Actually supported a few 101ˢᵗ Black Hawks. Had to recover a 101st Black Hawk that had trashed all four of the main rotor blade tip caps from striking a tree. Removed all four tip caps and flew it back to the Muskogee Airfield. Some were not too pleased with that, but it worked and saved a shit-load of time and maintenance. Our Little Birds were equipped with a set of sensors that would light lights and sound alarms if you were hit with simulated small arms, rockets, missiles, etc. The kits had never really been evaluated fully and on a test flight in the pattern, a device strapped to the plank flew off and struck the vertical fin of my aircraft. Scared the shit out of me and the engine mechanic I was flying with. Fucked up the vertical pretty bad. Incredibly lucky that it had hit the fin and not the tail rotor. About an inch between a hole in a fin and losing the tail rotor. Losing the tail rotor would have been very bad shit.

20-30 May deployed to Reno, Nevada. An uneventful trip, other than I lost about a hundred bucks gambling—something I never do—not losing, gambling. I'm not a gambler, or at least not a good one.

Had a flight in July in a Black Hawk with the guy from Green Platoon that had whipped my ass in Close Combat Skills. I only include this because this was the one time I was a recipient of a Flight OHR (Operational Hazard Report). An OHR is bad—potentially career-ending. I know, seems I'm always on the receiving end of career-ending shit. The OHR stated that I was engaging in flight aerobatics in the Black Hawk. Aerobatics are prohibited in Army helicopters. What had really happened was I had completed the in-flight test flight maneuvers I needed to do and asked my co-pilot Mike what else he thought needed to be checked out since this was a modification applied to our DAP (Defensive Armed Penetrator, fancy name for our armed Black Hawks) Black Hawk. He took the controls and performed a series of maneuvers to check out the sighting systems and other systems that could be affected by the modification. Turns out a 101st Huey was out in the Test Flight area and thought the maneuvers we were performing were aerobatics. The Huey pilots tracked me down through the Campbell Airfield base operations and filed the OHR. I could understand that since they were extremely aggressive and abrupt pull-ups and dives with turns requiring large angles of bank, steep climbs, and steep dives—normal maneuvers for us—not so much for a Huey. Upon return to the airfield, the 160th flight operations handed me the OHR. Luckily, I ran into a friend, Cliff Wolcott, who had pioneered the DAP Black Hawks as well as the maneuvers needed to attack targets. Cliff read the OHR and said, "I'll take care of this bullshit," and I never heard another word about it.

5- 30 August deployed to Ft. Bliss, Texas. Supporting another FTX. It was a joint exercise with all SOF (Special Operations Forces) elements playing games and was an exceptionally long, maintenance-intensive trip. Mostly just sucked.

19-26 September deployed to Ft. Bragg (Pope Air Force Base). I should explain. Pope and Bragg are pretty much co-located. We usually staged out of Pope supporting our Customers (Delta Force).

I know, secret and all that, but since "Black Hawk Down," the relationship between the Night Stalkers and Delta has become common knowledge. This trip was a train-up for a contingency to replace the guys deployed to Somalia. Not much on this trip except a few guys got drunk and flash banged (flash bangs are intensely bright and loud explosives) the battalion XO's (Executive Officer, a Major) hooch. Extremely amusing to all of us, not so much for the Major. Obviously, we never made that deployment.

I'm sure all have heard of the Battle of Mogadishu, Somalia, on 3 October. We lost five guys to two Black Hawk shootdowns (My friend Cliff Wolcott being one). One guy was captured. The bodies of our guys were dragged through the streets. Delta had two guys earn the Medal of Honor (posthumously). Several 160th pilots were awarded Silver Stars. As with battles before and since: "Uncommon valor was a common virtue." It was a terrible time. The unit held a memorial for our guys. Pam and I attended Cliff Wolcott's funeral held in Hopkinsville, Kentucky. Night Stalkers served as funeral detail for all the funerals in several different states. I will always feel the loss of those Night Stalkers.

Deployed to Duke Field, an airfield near Ft. Walton Beach, Florida, 1 thru 8 November. Another mostly boring trip except for one of our MH47 Chinook helicopters accidentally dumping a shit ton of fuel in their parking spot. Just as luck would have it, they were parked in a sod parking spot. Had to dig a damn hole to China to meet the EPA's clean-up requirements. They are always there to help, like the IRS (Internal Revenue Service) and the FAA (Federal Aviation Administration, whose motto should be "We're not happy until you're not happy"). Anyhow, that MH47 was thereafter dubbed the "Exxon Valdez," referring to the huge oil spill of 1989 (Google that for you young folks).

31 November to 3 December short trip to Duke Field again. Don't remember why. Did get my first deck landing qualification completed this trip on the USS Saipan.

"Feet Wet"

"Feet Wet" was the call when leaving the shoreline (used to ensure you checked equipment and settings for overwater flight). The "pucker factor" (the rate at which your asshole sucks up the seat bottom, applied to any tense situation) always goes up when the shoreline disappears. Being in a single-engine helicopter 50 feet above the water, you certainly appreciate the aircraft's radar altimeter and the dunker and HEEDS (Helicopter Emergency Egress Devise) training. HEEDS is a small bottle of oxygen worn during overwater flight along with "Water Wings," inflatable neck cushions. There are about three minutes of oxygen in the bottle. If you survived ditching or crashing, the plan is to ride out the crash, wait for the helicopter to roll over (all helicopters are top-heavy and will roll over), then get on your oxygen bottle, unbuckle, and make your way to the surface and inflate the water wings. If at any time you lost reference to which direction was up or where you were in the helicopter, you were fucked. That's why the dunker and HEEDS training were so important.

16 thru 23 November to Camp Lejeune, North Carolina. Based out of Cherry Point NAS and worked at an urban training site on Lejeune. Our enlisted guys were doing fast roping from the Little Birds when one of them fell off the edge of the third story of the building. Miraculously, he was basically ok--a few broken ribs, I think. We called an ambulance, and when they arrived, they cut off his uniform to fully evaluate him. Pissed him off. Deployed home single ship, single pilot. Not an issue usually, but this time, we had doors installed (we often did for cross-country admin flights). The doors were not well maintained and fit terribly since we seldom used them. My door came open, so I asked the guy I was flying with to take the controls while I closed the door. He warned me that he couldn't fly (he was a TI). I insisted he take the controls, and when he did, we nearly went upside down. Not good. Ended up landing in a field and shutting the door, which is what I should have done in the first damn place.

30 November to 1 December attended another engine school in Pleasantville, New Jersey. This was due to a contract change from Allison to a company named Airwork. Another great school. We went to Atlantic City one evening to see the sights, and I somehow

managed to drive the rent onto the Boardwalk. Yep, the actual wooden boardwalk. Looked like a bunch of redneck fools. Made a quick U-turn and got the hell out of there.

Deployed to Ft. Benning, Georgia, 13 to 16 December. Not sure what the mission was, not that it really ever mattered to us maintenance guys. We were there to fix broke helicopters. Period. That was always our number one mission. As a note, I flew down and back with my friend Carlos Guerrero—great guy who often drew the short straw and flew with us maintenance guys. Carlos was later killed in a crash during gunnery on our Range 29 back at Ft. Campbell. Carlos was a good dude.

10 thru 22 January 1994 to Dallas, Texas, for Urban Operations Support. The usual, except that I went on a ride along with a Dallas police officer. What a night. Transferred a prostitute to jail; she was trying to bum a cigarette even though she was in handcuffs. We were behind a Cadillac when they took off squealing tires. I thought, *What a dumbass; a cop behind you, and you do that?* So, chased them down the interstate at about 100 mph for several miles when the cop I was with suddenly backed off and started cussing. Turned out they were undercover guys. Special Ops Cops don't talk to regular cops much like us and regular Army guys. Got an "Officer in Trouble" code and responded to it immediately, along with every other police car in town, including a police helicopter overhead. They take that shit seriously. Turns out the guy had accidentally hit the emergency call button getting out of his car on a call. Shit happens. A cop's shift is much like flying—hours of boredom broken up by moments of terror.

Little Bird "Urban Operations"

26 February to 7 March to 29 Palms Marine Corp Training Base, California. Flew in the back of an MH-47 to a FARP (Forward Arming and Refueling site) to check on my Birds. One had a small hole in one of the tail-rotor blades, so I chose to fly it back to the airfield to replace the blade. It was about ten miles back to the airfield we were based out of. At about five miles out, the tail rotor picked up a high-frequency vibration. By the time we landed, it was bad. When we shut down, the small hole had turned into a big hole. Probably not the best call to fly it back.

4 thru 9 April to Ft. Bragg, North Carolina. Another "Dog and Pony Show."

15 thru 27 May to Ft. Rucker, Alabama, to attend The Aviation Safety Officer Course. I had been performing Safety Officer duties for F Company for quite some time but was not officially qualified. This school checked that block.

"IT'S FRIDAY. HERE'S YOUR WEEKEND SAFETY BRIEF . . .

DON'T BE A FUCKIN' IDIOT."

This was my weekend safety brief to my soldiers every Friday.

12 thru 18 June back to Ft Bragg, North Carolina.

13 thru 17 July to Savannah, Georgia.

25 July to Virginia Beach, Virginia. Only there one day when my brother Bob passed away. I had been expecting this, but it still was quite a shock. The Unit immediately got me a flight to Nashville, and I went on leave. Night Stalkers take care of each other.

21 thru 29 August to Los Angeles, California. Long-ass flight (about seven hours) in an AC-130 Air Force aircraft. Got to watch air-to-air refueling from the cockpit, which was quite interesting. LA was a fun place—lots to see and do. Took the required photos of the Hollywood sign from a Little Bird. Worked with the LA Air Unit and SWAT (Special Weapons and Tactics) folks. The LA police force is larger than most countries' armies.

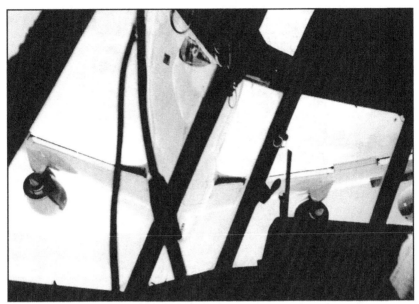

Air to air refueling as viewed from the cockpit of an AC-130
during the flight to Los Angeles.

Hollywood!

16 September deployed to Guantanamo Bay, Cuba, (called GITMO) as a Black Hawk MTP for two DAPs that would serve as an armed escort for a flight of ten Air Force MH-53 helicopters filled with Army Rangers for an assault on Haiti. The assault was called off at the very last minute as all helicopters were running and within seconds of take-off. With the mission canceled, I turned into a beach bum. I would drive our vehicle we called a "Mule" (small tactical trucks we used to haul equipment. We would stack a ton of equipment on those for uploading into Air Force transport aircraft. Thus, "Mule") down to the beach each morning to look for seashells and watch the iguanas.

The Mule, the beach, an iguana

Found many versions of small boats (or the remains of boats) washed on shore that the Haitians had tried (unsuccessfully) to use for the crossing to the US for asylum. I would not trust them to cross a farm pond, and they were attempting to cross about 100 miles of ocean. That's how bad conditions were in Haiti. Always wondered what became of the Haitians using those boats. Desperate people will try desperate things.

Boat washed up on shore at Guantanamo Bay, Cuba

Hangar living at GITMO. You ain't lived until you live in a
hangar with about 200 Army Rangers.

There were land crabs all over, many crushed on the roads.
"Banana rats" were everywhere. They looked like groundhogs—
harmless. 15 October, returned to Campbell.

15 November to Corpus Christi Army Depot in Texas to drop off
two of our old MH-60A model Black Hawks for turn-in. The Depot
would de-mod them back to regular Army helicopters and return
them to the regular Army fleet after a complete rebuild. Com Air
back to Nashville on the 16th.

On 2 December, I took a flight with my buddy Jim to turn in
a Black Hawk to BGAD (Bluegrass Army Depot) in Richmond,
Kentucky. Detoured to my hometown of Flemingsburg to visit my
father, who was dying of cancer. Pulled up to hover alongside the
house so Daddy could see us out the window. Waved and departed
towards Richmond. Not a big deal for me, but not a usual occurrence

for Flemingsburg, so it was quite an attention-getter I'm told. Turned into quite a story written by my brother, Garry, a published author. Check it out in his book titled *Kentucky Waltz.* He added a few fictional happenings to make the story more interesting, but the basic telling is true.

4 thru 12 December to Yuma Marine Corp Air Station, Arizona. A usual trip apart from an interesting encounter between an AH Little Bird and a Marine Corps "Fast Mover," as we called fixed-wing fighter aircraft. The Fast Mover was supposed to designate (with a laser) a target for the AH to launch a Hellfire missile to destroy the target. Well, the Fast Mover had flown out of its "box," protected airspace that assured the Hellfire would not see the laser and follow it towards the aircraft instead of towards the target, so the missile tracked to the Fast Mover. Fortunately, the missile was not a warhead (armed missile), so when it struck the aircraft, it did not explode but pierced through right behind the pilot's cockpit. Quite a hole in the aircraft but no damage to critical components that keep the aircraft flying. After many accusations from the Marine Corps it was proven the Marine pilot was at fault. The only time an AH6 helicopter nearly shot down a Marine fighter jet.

9 January 1995 thru 17 January to Ft. Benning, Georgia.

20 thru 25 February to Yakima Firing Center, Washington.

27 thru 29 March to Lakehurst, New Jersey. This is where the Hindenburg blimp crashed and burned. They have gigantic hangers that were used to house blimps--architectural wonders. This trip was to inspect the last Little Bird coming out of modification at the Lakehurst Naval Air Station Depot. Flew up in a Black Hawk. The trip started off interestingly enough. I was flying with a guy named

Mike, who was an Experimental Test Pilot (XP), which meant he was a graduate of the Navy Experimental Test Pilot Program, a mentally difficult program as well as requiring data-gathering flights in many different types of aircraft. Mike had not flown in a Black Hawk for some time and was probably not current (a flight in the last 60 days). Not my problem as I was not the PIC. We were flying the first leg on instruments as the weather was shit until the arrival time at the first fuel stop. As we began to enter the clouds (I was flying), ATC requested we "squawk" (broadcast from our transponder) the code they assigned us. Discovered Mike didn't know or could not remember how to perform this task, so I had to request to stay VFR (visual flight conditions) until we could transfer the controls and I could get the code entered into the transponder. A little embarrassing. Never assume the skills of your co-pilot regardless of his qualifications. I retook the controls and punched into the clouds. Uneventful flight after that to the next stop for fuel. When we went to crank the APU for shutdown, we discovered that the aircraft battery was completely drained. Flat. Dead. Had to perform a "dead" shutdown with no power to the aircraft, not something done unless absolutely necessary. We had no choice, so we completed the shutdown. The Black Hawk has what we call "idiot lights" to let the pilots know when the battery is low or has another type of problem. The light never came on, so this was why we had no clue until we landed. The next big problem was you could not crank a Black Hawk without either power from the APU or some external power source. The airport guys had nothing that would plug into the Black Hawk's external power receptacle. But they did have a cart with 24-volt batteries that were used to crank other aircraft. Decided to attempt to attach the jump battery to our aircraft battery. Had to disassemble the aircraft battery connector and hook the 24-volt battery to the connector with jumper cables. It worked, and we cranked the APU, got the aircraft started, and completed the flight to Lakehurst. The only time I have ever heard of starting a Black Hawk by jumping it like a car. Oh well, it worked.

While there got to take a flight along the Hudson River up past the Statue of Liberty and the Twin Towers. Now a bittersweet memory.

The Twin Towers from the cockpit of an MH-60 Black Hawk during a flight along the Hudson River

3 April thru 22 May I attended the MH-60K AQC at Ft. Campbell. It was quite a difficult course for me since this model Black Hawk was a huge step up in technology in the cockpit, being a "glass" cockpit. Beat my head against the dash for about ten hours of flight when one day, it was much like Alice walking through

the looking glass; everything just suddenly clicked. Nothing came to you. You had to go get everything by selecting the correct series/sequence of buttons. The joke was that one would fly for an hour with no one looking out of the cockpit. It was no joke. Spent about an hour once on the ramp at the airport at Richmond, Kentucky, while the IP tried to fix a flight plan software issue to make sure we had the correct flight commands for the flight back to Ft. Campbell. After an hour of useless button pushing, I suggested we fly home using a paper map (I could fly the route back to Campbell without a map after many flights between Richmond and Campbell). The IP was flabbergasted that we would fly home navigating with a paper map but finally agreed. Too much dependence on software.

The K Model was a great aircraft. (The K would later become the workhorse for assaults in Iraq and Afghanistan. It has since been replaced by the MH-60M). The K was a very heavy aircraft and required gentle handling to ensure power was available for takeoffs. At maximum gross weight, it was a pig. I flew with a civilian pilot from Sikorsky for the AQC course. Army IPs, when giving a simulated engine failure, would announce the simulated failure and slowly reduce power on one engine, mostly to ensure a safe and successful maneuver with no limitations exceeded. The Sikorsky IP would suddenly take one of the engine power levers to idle with no warning, and let you figure it out. I found that if you immediately decelerated the aircraft to the correct airspeed and watched your power, it was not an issue. Great training.

The initial version of the MH-60K had terrible software issues. The GPS had only one channel (as opposed to the nearly 20 channels used now). There was no database, so all target coordinates had to be what we called "finger fucked" or manually entered into the system. On a flight in the clouds, one crew inadvertently entered the checkpoint behind them as the next checkpoint. The software could only come up with one solution to get there, and that was to fly around the world. The entire system crashed, and they ended up with "blue screens" on all the cockpit displays. Not good, especially not good in the clouds. They managed to get down to visual flight conditions by using the old backup "steam gages," as we called them. Most of the software issues were corrected in later versions. Again, the K was a great helicopter. Just had the usual issues that are inherent to newly fielded aircraft of any kind.

In the MH-60K cockpit the "steam gauges" are located
in the dash between the displays.

30 May thru 20 June, attended the MH-60K MTP qualification course, also at Ft. Campbell. Not a whole lot different in test flight procedures between the K and our L models.

10 July thru 15 July to Pensacola NAS to support a K model train up for one of our companies that had transitioned to the K model. Had to return on the 15th to Campbell Com Air to fill a slot on the "Bullet." The "Bullet" was our ready-to-deploy package of personnel, helicopters, and equipment that was always on a four-hour, wheels-up recall.

31 July thru 4 August to Ft. Bragg, North Carolina. Another trip.

5 thru 9 September to Ft. Pickett, Virginia. One of many flights with my friend Jamie Weeks. Jamie was a hoot, country as fuck and funny as hell. Would tune the FM radio in the cockpit to a country station and usually never touch the controls.

28 and 29 September to Jacksonville, Florida, for dunker currency. Painfully necessary training.

24 October thru 6 November to Israel. Great trip. Initially locked down in an Israeli Air Force base. Had to get gas for the rent off the base one day, so loaded up all my guys in our van and headed to the Dead Sea. Figured, *what the hell*, we would get to see something while we were there. Completed the covert trip to the Dead Sea. That water is damn salty.

At the Dead Sea with my bottle of Dead Sea saltwater, I collected in an empty plastic Coke bottle. Still have it.

At the Wailing Wall in Jerusalem

Thought I had caused an international incident while we were at a range watching our Little Birds come and go for gas and ammunition. My head was leaning against the window of our rental van when someone knocked on the window. Without looking, I flipped the bird. When I looked up, there was an Israeli soldier there. I rolled down the window, thinking "Now I'm fucked." He said, "What is this?" returning the bird. I told him it meant "Hello." Quite sure, he knew what it meant. Fuck and such gestures are an international language spoken by nearly everyone. Never heard anything about it, so I guess an international incident was avoided.

After the training was completed, the restrictions were lifted, so we loaded up again and headed to Jerusalem. Found ourselves in a nasty part of town that we probably should not have been in with a wedding going on and a huge crowd of folks in the streets that did not appear to care for a van full of Americans. Made it through without incident. Jerusalem was a once-in-a-lifetime event. Toured the Church of the Holy Sepulchre. Visited the Wailing Wall. While there, one of the Jewish men was cranking his head up and down (Hey, it's what they do) when he received a call on his cellphone. He stopped his worship and answered the call. Would have been a great commercial for AT&T. The next day we traveled down to the Red Sea to the town of Eilat. Nothing about the town that stood out. Just wanted to see the Red Sea. The route to Eilat was through about two hours of desert. We came across a herd of camels in the road that were not at all fearful of a bunch of Americans in a van. One stuck his head into the van window and slobbered all over one of my guys. Good for a laugh.

Trying to be incognito (and failing badly) in Jerusalem.

GIs always stick out. I'm the bald guy.

20 November thru 17 November to New Orleans, Louisiana. Fun trip. If you haven't been to New Orleans, you should go there. We were hitting a target in a sleazy part of town, an old abandoned school building. The locals across the street had gathered on their porches, curious about all the activity and many police cars and officers about. (If possible, we tried to involve the local police to keep bystanders out of the area). This exercise started with a live sniper shot from one of our MH-6 Aircraft. Well, that certainly got their attention. The rest of the assault force of MH-60s and MH/AH-6s began to arrive on target, and one of the Black Hawk's rotor wash blew the roof off one of the shacks. That scattered the rest of the onlookers. The target scene gets loud, with small arms fire, flash bangs, and numerous helicopters. Usually, the unit would get several calls about the noise, sometimes resulting in us being asked to stop training. No calls here, or if there were, they were ignored. Nobody gives a shit about poor people living in shacks.

29 November thru 17 December to Panama. Another fun trip. I had been to Panama before, so I was familiar with the area. Driving a rent through Panama City is both terrifying and fun. Drive wide open and like an idiot, or you will be run over. There were certain areas of the city that we were advised to stay out of due to the locals still being pissed that we kicked their ass during the invasion of 1990. Took a wrong turn once and ended up in bad guy territory by myself in a flight suit. Not good. Managed to find my way out without incident. Monkeys hung out in the trees everywhere. At our FARP site at the range, they loved to get blown about by the Black Hawk's rotor wash. It was funny to see them begin to show up when we did, waiting for the ride. They also would throw shit at you (literally) if you happened to walk under a tree where they were hanging out. I think they thought it was fun. The Panama Canal was fascinating. How they change water levels in the locks is quite a feat of engineering. We would buzz the cruise ships coming through the locks just because we could.

AH-6 Little Birds over the Panama Canal.

While there flew an overwater route (NVG) with seas so calm that it was difficult to determine how high off the water you were. Trust that radar altimeter and the aircraft ahead of you. Training is the only way to gain that trust. Still the pucker factor was high.

We were staging out of Howard AFB, and one day my TI got pulled over by an MP. I pulled over to see what the problem was. The MP wanted to know who his CO was, so the TI told him I was. The MP handed the ticket to the TI, who then handed it to me. I wadded it up and threw it on the floorboard. Never heard anything about that ticket.

23 January 1996 thru 15 February to Virginia Beach, then on to Kuwait. From Kuwait, onto the USS Peleliu for a night, then onto the USS Denver. Floated around in the Persian Gulf on the Denver for six days, then back to Kuwait. From there, to Rota, Spain. This was a classified mission that got canceled after we arrived on the Denver. The guys trained for a few nights, anyhow. The Denver launched a drone aircraft each night before the helicopters launched. It took a rocket assist to get it off the deck. It was recovered prior to the helicopters returning, and they would erect a large net, much like a tennis net, and the drone operator would fly it into the net. The drone was propeller-driven, so the propeller would splinter in the net. This required a FOD (Foreign Object Damage) walk prior to the arrival of the helicopters. The Little Birds would recover first, followed by the Black Hawk. We had to quickly fold the Little Bird's main rotor blades, install the ground handling wheels, and push them inside a small shed-like room on deck to clear the landing spot for the Black Hawk. Not a big deal as we were well-trained in performing quick buildup and folding of our Little Birds. We berthed

in a vacant berthing area. The Navy takes fire training seriously but went to the extreme in running firefighting crews through our area every morning after we had been down for about an hour. I am positive it was designed to fuck with us Army invaders. It did. On the return trip to the US, we stopped in Rota, Spain. The C-5 Galaxy aircraft, a huge transport plane, was prone to breaking down and did. Spent three days showing up at midnight for roll call to be told the aircraft was still broken. We would return to the hotel and drink mass quantities. On the third day, my Avionics kid went to the crew to see if he could help in any way and fixed the problem (broken wire on a landing gear switch) in about 15 minutes. Think maybe the Air Force crew was getting in a little R&R (rest and relaxation).

7 April thru 15 April to Ft. Benning, Georgia. The usual there. Self-deployed to Alexandria, Louisiana, (Ft. Polk) on the 15th to play games in the training box there. The 17th was my birthday, and one of my guys snuck me a bottle of booze—much appreciated. Returned to Ft. Campbell 21 April.

31 May thru 7 June to Pittsburgh, Pennsylvania. Trained one night and was asked to stop training due to noise complaints. We were listening to a local radio station while the hit was going on (around 2 am), and who were up at that time besides the drunks and druggies. It was hilarious to hear them call in about bombs being dropped and such. One guy claimed it sent his wife into labor.

17 July thru 5 August to Savannah, Georgia. This was a deployment to support the 1996 Olympics in Atlanta as a contingency force in case of terrorist attacks. Funny thing that an attack was made while we were there (Centennial Olympic Park Bombing), and we never launched a single aircraft. Always enjoyed flying in the Test

Flight area around Hunter AAF, which was mostly over a swamp leading out into the Gulf. Lots of alligators to see. All that deployed were awarded the "Military Outstanding Volunteer Service Medal." Don't know why; I damn sure as hell never volunteered for this trip. We called it the "Beer Drinking Award" relating to an incident involving the illegal consumption of alcohol. We were denied alcohol use for the entire deployment due to being on call 24 hours a day. Nearly everyone ignored this but the F Company CO, who was just anal. Anyhow, near the end of the deployment, a couple of other MTPs and I decided we were through playing by the rules that only F Company was following, so we bought a six-pack of tallboys for consumption in our hotel room. Said anal F Company CO walked in, had a fit, and lectured for hours on the evil we were perpetrating. Hence, the "Beer Drinking Award."

5 October thru 31 October to Fort Indiantown Gap, Pennsylvania, to attend the Little Bird IP Course. This course trained pilots to conduct emergency procedure training with other pilots and conduct evaluations as well. Many, many autorotations every day. Classroom instruction on half of the days, with flight in the aircraft the other half. Fun course of instruction. Took my end-of-course check ride with CW5 Randy Jones, a true legend in the 160th. The man can flat-out fly a Little Bird. Learned quite a bit on that ride, which is a large part of any evaluation to teach...at least; that is my take on it. Passed an eight-hour oral evaluation the day prior to the check ride. Turned out I was never a good IP. My niche was always test flying. I was good at that, and I had developed a sort of sixth sense when pre-flighting and flying to find shit wrong or sense impending failures.

Drove to Hershey to see the chocolate factory. While there, hot air balloons began to ascend near the factory, so I pulled over and watched. I saw every kind and shape of hot air balloon known to man. Pretty damn fascinating. Hot air balloon festivals are cool.

3 December thru 14 December to El Centro, California, then to North Island NAS to the USS New Orleans. Spent seven days floating, then back to North Island, then back to Ft. Campbell on the 14th. Had my first encounter with severe turbulence on the flight from El Centro to San Diego. Scared the shit out of me. Felt like a giant was slapping the helicopter. We returned to El Centro, called up a C-141 transport aircraft, and flew to North Island NAS courtesy of the Air Force. Something different for this trip was I rode the ship back into dock at San Diego. Kind of neat coming into the bay.

Coming into San Diego Bay at dawn on board the USS New Orleans.

13 January 1997 to "Rosy Roads" (Roosevelt Roads NAS), Puerto Rico. Flew out to Vieques Island each day for gunnery and would return after night gunnery. The water was about 50 to 75 feet deep and crystal clear all the way to the bottom. Really beautiful. They

put us up in a resort on the beach—hard living. Shared a bungalow with a couple of other MTPs. Great trip. Returned the 25th.

I was promoted to CW4 in February. Glad to finally pin that rank on. No more SDO, and I usually would get my own rent and room on trips.

CW4 promotion by Pam and the F Company CO.

24 February to 7 March to Charleston, South Carolina. Based out Charleston International. Flew to Charlotte, North Carolina, to conduct urban ops. Got in one rehearsal and one mission before they kicked us out. The Charlotte mayor claimed he had been "hoodooed" by Army guys in civilian clothes. Probably he said this to cover his ass. We always sent our intelligence guys to brief the local mayors, police, and anyone else that needed to be read-on to what we were doing, so they always knew about the noise and potential for complaints.

After the mission night, the flight home got very interesting. About halfway back to Charleston, we encountered shit weather and were forced to land. We were a flight of three and landed in the only well-lit area we could see. The weather was down to about zero visibility by the time we got on the ground. The version of Little Bird we flew was not legally equipped to fly in the clouds, so we were forced to land. (The Black Hawks just punched into the clouds and flew back to Charleston on instruments.) The lights were extremely bright, so we wondered what kind of facility this was. We shut down and gathered to formulate a plan for the night. A van approached us, and a couple guys got out of it. Two of our guys approached them and were immediately advised by the guys from the van to stop, place their identification on the ground, and back away. These guys were not bullshitting, as they were armed with shotguns and pistols. Our guys were wearing what we call our "Kit," which was an armored vest and an array of survival equipment. We were unarmed as this was a training exercise, but I'm guessing we looked pretty threatening to prison guards. That's right, we had landed next to a prison, and the guards were not pleased, to say the least, thinking we were going to bust someone out. When they figured out that we were good guys that needed a place to stay, they really took care of us. Took us for a tour of the prison (it was around 2 am), loaded us into a prison van, and hauled us to a nearby Air Force base to spend the night. Even guarded our helicopters. What started out badly turned out well. We flew back to Charleston the next morning. Returned to Ft. Campbell 7 March.

6 April thru 2 May attended the Warrant Officer Staff Course at Ft. Rucker. Mostly a huge waste of time writing a bunch of papers and sitting in boring classes. It was interesting to attend with warrant officers of other MOSs since, generally, aviation warrants only interact with other aviation warrants. Got to hang out with a couple friends from flight school, which was cool.

6 May thru 10 May to Ft. Bragg, North Carolina. Don't remember why.

18 June thru 25 June to Aberdeen Proving Grounds, Maryland. Uneventful trip. Ate some great seafood. Took a flight along the Chesapeake Bay and Susquehanna River, an incredibly beautiful part of the US.

Except for a five-day trip to Mother Rucker 2 thru 6 September, for some reason, I was at Ft. Campbell in July, August, and September. Could be the longest time period at home since I joined the 160th.

20 October thru 30 October to Albuquerque, New Mexico. I went to support internal training as well as supporting what is now known as SOATB (Special Operations Aviation Training Battalion). Back then, they were designated S&T (Selection and Training Company). They had deployed for desert training, and we happened to be there together; no use in having two MTPs deployed, so I covered the SOATB aircraft also. Uneventful trip.

November and December at home. Awarded Master Army Aviator wings on 15 December, a huge milestone in an aviator's career. The requirement for Master Wings was 2,000 flight hours and 15 years of aviation service. I had the 15 years and well over 3,000 hours by then.

10 January 1998 thru 31 January to Ft. Hunter-Liggett, California. Got called downrange to evaluate an AH-6 that had reported a bird strike. Arrived on scene and discovered a large rock had broken the pilot's side windshield. Bird strike my ass. The AH-6s would always shoot very close to the target and would habitually pick up holes in windows, tail rotor, and main rotor blades, either from rocks, minigun brass, or rocket motor shrapnel. A huge part of my time was spent tracking and balancing the main rotor and tail rotor blades that were replaced after a gunnery.

17 thru 20 February to Ft. Bragg, North Carolina. Again, I do not remember why.

23 February thru 27 February to BGAD.

13 March thru 31 March, a long-ass trip starting at Ft. Lewis, Washington, for eight days, then to Edwards Air Force Base, California, for two days, then to North Island NAS, then out to the USS Boxer for seven days, and then back to Edwards and then back to Ft. Campbell. Do not remember a lot about the trip other than it was just long. I guess not much happened.

Me and my guys on the deck of the USS Boxer. I'm the bald guy...again.

17 May thru 22 May, another New Orleans trip. Uneventful. My last trip with the unit before retirement.

Last flight as an Army pilot (before my first retirement) was a test flight 17 July in an MH-60K.

August and September were at Ft. Campbell. It takes time to retire. Tons of appointments for everything from finance to transportation. I had to clear damn near every entity and office on post, getting the coveted stamp on my clearing papers. Had to clear CIF (Central Issue Facility). That was a goat fuck. I had equipment issued to me from my arrival at Ft. Campbell in January of 1988, so some of it had been in boxes for a long time. Decided to take a "statement of charges" for my flight helmet bag, the original one from flight school. Cost me around 25 bucks, I think. Had to clear the 160th OCIE (organizational clothing and individual equipment) Another goat fuck, as the 160th issues a shit ton of equipment. Had to do a "statement of charges" for a five-gallon water bag. I asked who in the unit is issued two five-gallon water bags (I had one), and the answer was, "Nobody," so I said, "How in the hell then would I have been issued two of them?" Ended up paying for it in the end. Final clearance was 11 September. Started leave on the 12th. F Company hosted my retirement ceremony inside the F Company hangar on 16 October. Nice ceremony. Glad my mom, sister Bonnie, my mother-in-law, Jewell, and sister-in-law Rhonda could attend, as well as my daughter, Kerry, and wife, Pam, of course. Had to give a retirement speech, which I hated as I am not a good public speaker. But, got through it ok. Wish I had kept a copy of what I said.

CW4 Barker giving retirement speech, 1998

There were countless birthdays, anniversaries, holidays, and other special occasions missed due to deployments. When telling others of an event or occasion, Pam usually starts with the disclaimer," Jon was deployed, of course."

I was home for my daughter's graduation and her marriage. She married Billy, her high school sweetheart, a really great guy. She attended Austin Peay University in Clarksville, Tennessee, where she completed her degree in teaching. She and Billy were married shortly after both graduated from Austin Peay, and they moved to Memphis, Tennessee. Billy attended the University of Tennessee Memphis to complete a degree in dentistry. Kerry taught in Shelby County, one of the poorest counties in Tennessee. They lived on her meager teacher's salary until Billy completed his dentistry degree. While they lived in Memphis, they traveled to Russia to adopt our grandson, Alex. I have never seen a braver couple: to travel to Russia and face the uncertainty of the weather, travel accommodations, money issues, and an extremely hostile Russian court system. They returned later to adopt our granddaughter Karoline and have since had a home-made grandchild, Kate. I am extremely proud of them.

I know I have bored you with the listed deployments but wanted to be sure the enormous amount of time spent away from home was documented. I am sure I missed a few deployments. The constant demands of training and real-world missions were a hardship for my family. I will always be grateful for the support of my wife and daughter.

If you noticed very few pictures from my 160th days. As a rule, we did not take photos of our operations or helicopters for operational security reasons. Plus, back then, we used cameras not cell phones.

Threw me a retirement party in October. Fun time. 1 November 1998, I officially retired from the Army. 23 Years, 2 Months, 2 Days.

Retirement cake Pam had made for me.

12.

1998 THRU 2007 AT FT. CAMPBELL

I went to work for DynCorp on 2 November. No break in the action. DynCorp was the company that held the civilian contract for maintenance for the 160th. We were a bit guilty of nepotism, but it was really the only way to get qualified pilots to support the maintenance contract. I was still flying MH-60s and Little Birds. The entire year of 1999, I flew my ass off but was mostly at home except for an occasional trip to BGAD. 29 March thru 8 April I covered an S&T trip to Hurlburt Field, Florida, for overwater training for the Green Platoon pilots. Deployed to Kirkland Air Force Base, New Mexico, with S&T 6 July thru 16 July for desert training. 24 July thru 30 July to Hurlburt Field again. 8 November thru 16 November back to Hurlburt. It did not take much for my transition to being a civilian pilot since the only thing that changed was I no longer deployed with the Unit guys.

January of 2000, short trip to Ft. Eustis, Virginia, to test fly an aircraft being used for testing there. Remember it snowed about four inches—unusual for that area. Several trips to BGAD during the year. 27 March thru 6 April back to Hurlburt 10 July thru 21 July to Albuquerque, New Mexico for desert training. 31 July thru 10

August to Pensacola NAS, Florida, for overwater training. Returned 27 November thru 7 December to Pensacola for more of the same.

2001 started off the same, with lots of flying. 5 March thru 15 March back to Albuquerque. 8 May thru 18 May to Ft. Benning. 9 July thru 20 July to Albuquerque.

Then came September 11, 2001. I was at BGAD with a bunch of other pilots and maintainers attending classes on the latest model of Little Bird, the M Model. We were all horrified by what we saw. We were pissed. We knew the world would never be the same. It has not been.

2002 was uneventful for me. The 160th went to war. I was frustrated by not being able to deploy with them. Finished my A/MH-6M pilot and MTP qualification. It was a formality, as I had been performing ground runs for some time at BGAD. The first time I started an M Model, I had never had any formal training, so I just figured it out and hoped I wouldn't break anything. The M flies much the same as the J Model , so no problem there. There definitely was a lack of communication between the fielding team and us MTPs. We were flying the helicopter above 150 knots on a regular basis until they informed us the maximum airspeed was 130 knots. Oops! Cannot do something you don't know about. Same with autorotation airspeed. We were using the same as the J Model . Turns out that was also about ten knots slower than what was required. Would have been great to know that in case an actual in-flight failure required an autorotation. The damn M Model autorotated like a brick, anyhow.

8 July thru 18 July to Albuquerque, NM. 2 December thru 12 December to Pensacola, FL. That was all for 2002.

In March 2003, I began to travel to BGAD on a regular basis. The M Models were beginning to flow off the modification line, and they were being fielded to the Unit. I began to average around two weeks a month at BGAD.

21 April thru 26 April deployed to Ft. Bragg with the MH guys to see what, if any, capabilities were improved with the M compared to the J. The M had much more power, so the MH guys were able to increase their payload. This would give them more riders on the plank, so more combat capability on the battlefield.

Three weeks in May, I was at BGAD. I always came home on the weekends. I would drive up on Monday and return on Friday.

Seven days in June to BGAD.

10 thru 16 August to Ft. Benning. I was beginning to deploy with the Unit on training trips since the F Company MTPs were spending so much time deployed to Iraq. When they were home, they had no desire to deploy on training trips, and I certainly didn't blame them. I enjoyed deploying with the Unit again, even if only on training trips.

31 August thru 5 September to Virginia Beach. Overwater training.

22 thru 26 September to BGAD. October had eight days at BGAD.

In November, I was gone for three days somewhere. Don't remember where or why.

January 2004 had ten days at BGAD.

17 thru 25 February to Ft Lewis. Another trip with the Unit. AH guys this time for gunnery with the Rangers.

12 thru 15 March, I deployed to the Atlanta Motor Speedway. Great trip. The MH guys performed an infill inside the track for a

race day demonstration. Really a fun time. They treated us great. Free food, beer, and NASCAR race.

22 thru 31 March to Key West, Florida. MH and AH guys for overwater training. While conducting overwater extraction training, one of our AH crew chiefs drowned. It was a reminder that the routine training we do every day is not routine. It is extremely dangerous. We are so used to it that all training seems routine. It was a shit trip after that. The AH guys stopped training and returned to Ft. Campbell. The MH guys continued to train. The crew chief's body was recovered two days after he drowned.

April had eight days at BGAD.

3 thru 10 May to El Paso, Texas, for Unit Desert and Mountain training in the Model M. Uneventful trip.

July and August 21 days at BGAD.

16 thru 22 October back to Virginia Beach. Overwater training.

Eight days at BGAD in November.

January 2005 had 17 days at BGAD.

March 15 thru 21st another trip to Atlanta Motor Speedway. Another great trip. Same treatment as before. NASCAR loves the military.

Seven days at BGAD in April.

2 thru 6 May to Phoenix, Arizona, to the Boeing Plant. Trip to test fly a Little Bird undergoing flight testing.

Eight days at BGAD in May.

June thru October 27 days at BGAD.

13 thru 16 November in Rochester, New York. Training trip with the MH guys. If you think Kentucky and Tennessee have hillbillies, you ain't seen upstate New York. Holy Shit! They make us Kentucky

hillbillies look like city folk. I am not shittin' you. Trip ended early for me as a tornado struck our subdivision in Clarksville. I com aired home immediately. Pam had ridden out the tornado in the basement garage with the cats for company. Minimal actual damage to the house; the roof had to be replaced, and the soffit was ripped off. This allowed pink insulation to be sucked out and pasted all over the house and lawn. Laid my flagpole flat on the ground. Blew our lawn furniture all over the place. Scared the shit out of Pam and the cats.

Two more days at BGAD in November.

Two days at BGAD in January 2006.

16 thru 28 January in Dahlgren, Virginia. Supported electromagnetic testing on a M Model. It was extremely boring. Crank at 0700, run at idle for four hours while being subjected to all types of electromagnetic frequencies, take lunch, run for another four hours. Fried a few of the helicopter avionics components. Hard to tell what kind of health problems that caused. (I returned to Dahlgren again later for another few weeks of the same but can't remember when.)

February thru April 21 days at BGAD.

Six days at BGAD in May. Traveled on Monday the 15th. Was informed around 9 am on the 16th that my friend Jamie Weeks had been killed in a helicopter shootdown in Iraq on Mother's Day, the 14th. Horrible news. Jamie had been at BGAD quite a bit working on the M Model fielding, so we had spent a lot of time together there (as well as Ft. Campbell). Another sad funeral for Pam and I. Enforced my feeling that I needed to be contributing to the war effort. At least I was delivering safe, mission-ready helicopters to the Unit so that they could take the fight to the enemy.

The badge in the picture below is one I used to get into the BGAD compound. Jamie took me outside the hangar one day and said, "Stand your ass right there," took the picture and said, "Your ass needs a fuckin' badge since you're up here so much." He was right. I cherish that badge now. Miss his country ass.

4 days at BGAD in June.

Ten days at BGAD in July.

Thirteen days at BGAD in August.

Three days at BGAD in September.

Twelve days at BGAD in October.

Five days at BGAD in November.

28 November thru 10 December to Savanna, Georgia.

8 thru 12 January 2007 at BGAD.

22 thru 24 January at BGAD. It was during this trip that I went cross-eyed. Yep, batshit cross-eyed. Scared the shit out of me, thought that I was having a stroke. My friend Brock took me to the local hospital in Richmond. They performed a CAT scan, and a doc checked me out. He could find no sign of a stroke, so sent me to a local eye doctor. He checked me out and diagnosed me with 6th nerve palsy. I asked what the hell that was. He said a problem with the 6th nerve. No shit. I asked how long I would be cross-eyed, and he said around six months for the symptoms to disappear. Bought an eye patch. Found I could wear the patch on either eye, which seemed weird. Traveled back to Ft. Campbell, was immediately grounded of course. Went on short-term disability to wait out the symptoms. Being cross-eyed is no fun. Depth perception is fucked. Driving and about everything else was challenging. I could see ok from either eye if one of them was covered. Had to wear the eye patch all the time, so people generally stared at me. One kid at the Ft. Campbell commissary blurted out," Look, Mommy, a Pirate," and the mom about shit herself with embarrassment. Did not bother me; I thought it was funny. I had seen an eye doc at Blanchfield Hospital on Ft. Campbell, but he agreed it was 6th nerve palsy until one day, on a routine follow-up, my eye pressure had skyrocketed. He hand-carried me down for an MRI. The MRI showed nothing. He then asked if I would be willing to go to Vanderbilt Hospital in Nashville for an arterial gram, a type of test that would show a live or moving picture of what was going on in my head. He suspected I had a fistula, or brain bleeding of some kind. At that point, I was willing to do whatever it took to fix my eyes, so in about a month or so, I was at Vanderbilt for the procedure. I was mildly sedated for the procedure, so I heard the

neurologist say that I had a huge bleed. Turned out to be a "carotid cavernous fistula, "a rather large one evidently. The bleeding caused the veins in my sinus area around my eye to swell, and one of them had swollen enough that it was rubbing on my 6th nerve, causing the cross-eyed condition. During a consult with the neurologist, he explained that he would be taking one of three routes to my brain to stop the bleeding. The preferred route was through the carotid artery, the next would be through a notch in my skull behind my eye, and the third was through my skull. I was shocked that this could require my skull to be cracked open for access to the bleeding. He was not a bit concerned about this; he said he routinely performed this type of surgery, not on my head, though. I was concerned, but not enough to not opt for the surgery. A week or so prior to the scheduled surgery, my cross-eyedness went away. I called the doc to report this, wondering if I would still need the surgery. He said, "If that fistula fixed itself, you and I are going on tour as a freakshow." I guessed correctly that I would still need the surgery. About a week prior to the scheduled surgery, he called and said that after consulting with another neurologist (a Dr. Miracle, the doctor I had asked for originally... wouldn't you? I mean "Doctor Miracle") that they would be taking the route through the eye notch. They had arranged for a world-renowned eye surgeon to cut the eyelid back because of the many nerves in that area, and she routinely performed surgeries requiring cosmetic surgery cuts in that area. On my birthday, April 17th, I was once again headed for the operating table. The procedure took over eight hours but was a success. Later in a follow-up with the eye surgeon, she said that when the neurologist began to fill the veins with whatever they used to stop the bleeding, the cloudiness in the camera pictures began to disappear, as if an eraser was erasing the cloudiness. I would require two more arteriograms to confirm there was no more bleeding. One in May and another in June.

25 June, I returned to work with DynCorp. 19 July, I passed the required check rides and was back in the cockpit. I did require a waiver from Mother Rucker's Flight Doctors to continue to fly, but it was not a problem.

As a side note; I had been chopping away on my master's degree with Embry Riddle. One master's level class was considered full-time by the VA (Veterans Administration), so I only took one class at a time and actually was pocketing a few bucks from the VA for the first time. Finally completed the last of the requirements and was awarded a Master of Aeronautical Science degree, with a secondary of Aviation/Aerospace Safety Systems Specialization. I attained all my degrees using my GI Bill entitlement, and not one hour was earned prior to 1700 hours (5 pm for you civilians). All completed after regular duty hours. It had taken a lot of hard work, dedication, and some understanding commanders along the way. It was also a huge pain in the ass—just to say so.

30 July thru 3 August I was back at BGAD.
13 thru 17 August to BGAD.
15 thru 19 October at BGAD.
21 thru 26 October at BGAD.
29 October thru 2 November at BGAD.
6 thru 9 November at BGAD.

Another chapter in my life was about to begin. Two of the aircraft I had delivered to Ft. Campbell in November had gone to the SOATC Battalion. I was called into the DynCorp office by my bosses to be told that those helicopters were of a sub-standard quality of maintenance on delivery. I was pissed. The list of gigs (faults) was total bullshit. Someone was on a vendetta to ruin my reputation. I was sure who it was but could not prove it. I was also extremely disappointed that none of my co-workers or friends stood up for me. Oh well, you find out who your friends really are in situations like these. So, the Army was at war, the 160th needed test pilots, and there was a program that allowed retired warrant officer pilots to return to active duty. I was fed up with DynCorp and its losers, so guess what I chose? Pam was not particularly pleased but knew that I had wanted to get in the fight. After my cross-eyed experience, she figured I deserved a chance to do just that.

Back to the 160th...

13.

VOLUNTARY RETURN TO ACTIVE DUTY 2007 THRU 2014 AT FT. CAMPBELL

On 7 December 2007, I returned to active duty as a CW4. It was a little bizarre at first. I called my uniform a "costume" since I felt like I was really dressing for a play I was acting in. Cell phone this time instead of a beeper. I thought it would be a good gig being just a test pilot. I was once again issued the shit ton of equipment I had turned in in 1998, plus a shit ton more since the war was on. I did not have to take any check rides as nothing had changed when I returned to active duty. I was just an F Company MTP, but not for long. Soon the need arose for an SIP and an ME in F Company, and I was the logical pilot to fill those shoes. In February, I took the necessary check rides to be the F Company SIP/MTFE. So much for the easy life I was hoping for.

On 18 March 2008, I deployed to Germany en route to Iraq. The next 66 days would be in Balad, Iraq, a joint-use airbase about 40 miles north of Bagdad. Balad was, by most standards, a pretty nice place to be. We (Special Operations) had our own compound with our own mess hall, living quarters, shower, latrine, etc. I lived inside an Iraqi covered aircraft bunker, and by covered, I mean many feet of concrete, already tested by numerous bombs prior to our takeover of the airfield. We had a large contingent of aircraft on site, enough to conduct day and night operations against the numerous targets in the area. I worked mostly days, test flying aircraft that had been repaired or at the completion of scheduled maintenance. Never liked having my helicopters out at night with me not watching "kill TV," our nickname for the visual feed of missions provided by overhead assets. During the day, if a mission launched, I would be at the TOC (Tactical Operations Center) so that if an aircraft went down for maintenance or enemy action, I would be able to assess the situation and get my DART (Downed Aircraft Recovery Team) alerted and ready to execute a battlefield recovery, either by repairing the helicopter on site or rigging it for sling load by Black Hawk back to Balad. Watching the operations in real time was interesting, to say the least. Watched a lot of "bad guys" sent to Allah courtesy of our guys. I will just let that go at that.

The chow was decent; I had my own room and discovered our latrines were co-ed; quite a surprise when I was taking a piss and in walked an Air Force female. Nobody had clued me in, so I got used to it. The first two weeks I had another MTP on site to show me how day-to-day operations went (other than co-ed latrines, I guess), so that made it somewhat easier. After about a week at Balad, we deployed to another site where we kept a small number of Little Birds to support the customers' operations nearer to BIAP (Bagdad International Airport). That place was a shithole. The wood used to construct the barracks there had been soaked in some nasty shit that made your eyes burn. In the traffic pattern just outside of where our helicopters were staged was a trash dump (burn pit) that constantly burned anything dumped in it, which along with the birds that hung out by the thousands, created a hellish environment to work and fly in. The traffic pattern required dodging birds and smoke, and if the flight required altitude, it was necessary to enter the inner racetrack pattern at BIAP. This was dreamed up by some moron on drugs. Trying to conduct a test flight inside the pattern (literally, it was an oblong pattern between BIAP's two main runways) at BIAP, which was constantly full of fast movers, C-5 and C-17s and any other type of aircraft you could think of was quite an adventure. The ATC (Air Traffic Controllers) barely had control over the US aircraft and mostly no control over the international flights and coalition aircraft. Head on a swivel, as they say. Spent about four days there and returned to Balad. The routine became: get up, check the status board for any maintenance updates, hit the gym for about an hour, shower, hit the flight line usually until dark. I would always be on hand to launch all missions before heading to the TOC, so launching the AH Little Birds for their night mission usually ended my day. We had beepers to alert us to unscheduled missions, which usually worked. Missions were driven by Intelligence Surveillance and Reconnaissance (ISR) aircraft. (Overhead Visual Observation Platforms, which could be fixed-wing or unmanned, and were on station 24 hours a day). One such mission happened on Easter morning, 27 April. Early morning missions were unusual, but the intel put these targets in a prime spot for interdiction. I watched the action from the TOC. These Bad Guys were not smart and chose to shoot at our helicopters, which ended badly for them. I watched as their bodies were searched and left lying beside their hooptie. Great way to start Easter Day. Bad Guys didn't take holidays off. We didn't either.

Another time the guys were tracking a hooptie with known Bad Guys in it, waiting for a window of opportunity to interdict the target. This was usually a stretch of road where they could be isolated in an attempt to control collateral damage. They were approaching a bridge that, if they crossed it, would put them into an urban area where the interdiction could not be performed. The chatter had been about what was in the back of the hooptie, as the ISR feed could not get a clear view of what it was. Anyhow, the decision was made to hit the target before they crossed the bridge. A pair of AH Little Birds rolled in, and the lead bird hit the hooptie with a minigun, and holy shit! The secondary explosion was tremendous. Guessed propane tanks were in the back of the hooptie. Interdiction complete.

Many of the shitheads that were rolled up off the targets had been collected in a prior interdiction. They would be interrogated and usually released. One such pair evidently knew the drill from their prior interdiction, so when the black helicopters appeared alongside them, they stopped, got out, and proceeded to remove their clothing. Scared naked, I guess. They were not ready to meet Allah just yet. Pretty funny.

Mortar attacks were usually about every three days or so. They never hit anything of importance, at least while I was there. Just a nuisance.

On 28 April, I had the pleasure of conducting a Combat DART. I was at the TOC as usual when one of the pilots reported a problem with his helicopter's engine components. After some discussion back and forth, it was decided that we could not repair the aircraft on the battlefield and would have to sling the aircraft by Black Hawk back to Balad. I had already alerted my DART Team, so we were able to board the recovery Black Hawk quickly and headed to the downed aircraft site. (We trained for DART Missions constantly, so we had a package with all the equipment needed ready to go.) At the downed aircraft site, we offloaded, set security, and proceeded to rig the helicopter for sling load. It was around midafternoon and was about in the mid-90s heat range. Each of the DART Team members was responsible for a specific task to get the downed helicopter rigged for sling load. One of my guys and I were tasked with moving a package we had rigged on a two-wheeled cart, which turned out to be a terrible idea when trying to move it in a field that had been prepared for irrigation at some point and was lined with ditches set about four feet apart. It was quite a workout for my old ass, as well as the young soldier assigned to assist me. We finally were able to move the cart to the aircraft, and the team began to rig it for sling load. The security for us was provided by the customers—normally. This time our security guys loaded back up on a Black Hawk to conduct a target hit near us. No idea who made that call; it was well above my head, but it left us alone on the battlefield with only me and my DART Team Members—five guys total. We could hear the actions on the target (explosions, gunfire), which were very nearby, so we finished rigging the Little Bird for sling load and waited for our ride home to return. As all this was happening, we were rapidly running out of daylight and decent weather, so it became a race to get the aircraft on the sling under a Black Hawk and get back to Balad. I was not a fan of spending the night in Bad Guy country, even though we were equipped and prepared to do so. The guys hit three targets while we were on the ground, so they were happy campers. We did get the Little Bird sling loaded back to Balad just as the sun went down and the weather went to shit, so it was a successful Combat DART Mission. Caught the rotator flight on 23 May back to Germany en route to Ft. Campbell.

Spent about ten days at BGAD between June and August. Went to Colorado Springs, Colorado, with the AH guys for a week at the end of August. Four days at Virginia Beach, Virginia, in September.

Another great NASCAR trip in October, this time to Kansas City, Kansas. I rode on the plank of an MH-6 for the flyby. The crowd was so loud I could not hear the sound from the Little Bird's rotor and engine, absolutely incredible.

I took this picture while riding on the plank en route to conduct a flyby at the Kansas City Raceway. Unusual to have MH-6, MH-60, and MH-47 helicopters in the same formation.

4 November, returned to Balad. Spent about a week at Q-West during this rotation, another shit-hole airfield we staged from at

times. I should add: good shit hole, as we were left alone by everyone. The ride to Q-West from Balad was a C-23 Sherpa Aircraft (a squirrely small boxy airplane I did not like) that served as a nightly taxi for troops needing to get to various locations throughout Iraq. This one included stops at Mosul, Erbil, and Q-West. Rotated out of Balad and arrived back at Campbell on 5 December.

February of 2009 to New Orleans, Louisiana, for ten days. Staged out of a Coast Guard Station this time. Good trip.

22 thru 27 February to Ft. Benning. Do not remember this trip, so I assume nothing significant happened.

In March, deployed to Puerto Rico, then from there to the Dominican Republic via C-130 for a target hit. Spent a couple nights in a hangar on an airfield there. C-17 back to Campbell was delayed. Surprise, surprise. Money guy bought pizza, beer, and local rum for morale purposes. Morale was high those nights.

18 May rotated to Iraq/Balad. Made another trip to Q-West this rotation to give a new MTP a familiarization with the area. Arrived back at Campbell 19 June.

11 July departed Ft. Campbell for Yakima, Washington. Deployed to Ft. Lewis, Washington, 17 July, returned to Ft. Campbell 27 July.

8 thru 12 September to Virginia Beach, Virginia.

25 thru 30 October to Yakima, Washington.

8 January 2010 deployed en route to Kandahar, Afghanistan. This would begin a couple of years of bouncing between Iraq and Afghanistan. Kandahar, at the time, was a huge airfield with US, British, German, and several other countries' forces stationed there. One of the advantages of having coalition forces at Kandahar was each country had its own mess hall but allowed anyone to eat there.

We had an Asian night, British night, Belgium night, German night. You get the picture.

We encountered a problem with pilots reporting running out of aft cyclic—not good (aft cyclic is used to slow or stop the helicopter). We checked and rechecked the aircraft's cyclic rigging and anything else that could be related to an aft cyclic rigging problem and found no issues. I ran into this problem myself when repositioning an AH from our ramp to another ramp for up-load into a C-130 aircraft for transport to Kunduz, another location where targets were presenting themselves on a regular basis. Anyhow, while repositioning at takeoff, I realized I had run out of aft cyclic; I recovered the helicopter before crashing it and found that with my back armor plate in my vest, I would indeed run out of aft cyclic. I unbuckled, pulled my back armor plate out, handed it to the crew chief in the left seat, and then proceeded down to the load-out ramp. (I had also lost cockpit communication with the crew chief, so he thought I had lost my mind). The front of our vest is loaded with extra ammo magazines for our M-4 rifles and 9MM pistol, and about anything else one believed necessary to have strapped to his body for flight in Bad Guy country. The fix to the aft cyclic problem--lose the back armor plate or lessen the amount of shit strapped to the vest, so it was out with the back armor plate, which was not such a big deal as the helicopter seats had armor built into the seat backs or lose enough weight to accommodate the back armor plate. When discussing this with the AH Company Commander back at Campbell, his reaction was, "So you're telling me my pilots are fat?" This was funny only because he had an accent and a dry sense of humor that made it funny. Great guy, though. Think he made it to Two-star General. Returned to Kandahar after three days.

The rest of the trip was pretty much routine. The Bad Guys shot rockets at us there—weapon of choice, I guess. Did have a few rockets land close enough to rattle the windows in our hooptie. Kandahar had an elaborate alarm system which they tested around 0900 on Wednesdays. The test would wake me up and go on forever it seemed. They had a different alarm sound for a ground attack, rocket attack, etc. All sounded the same to me. Never served a practical purpose, as the attacks were over by the time the alarm went off. Always in sets of three rockets, so if you heard the first one, you knew two more were inbound. One night, my TI and I were eating chow in our maintenance tent (we usually got a plate to go) when we heard a rocket fly overhead. We looked at each other, and both of us said, "Well, two more to go." Sure enough, we heard two more go overhead and impact somewhere nearby and then finished our meal. There was a place in Kandahar called "the boardwalk" because there were shops around a square boardwalk Go figure. The Bad Guys knew troops would gather at the boardwalk and chow halls and tried to target them during the chow hours (another good reason for a plate to go).

There was one encounter with a couple of Sergeant Majors that finally clinched my decision never to go to a mess hall. The dinner meal was served during the hours of darkness (during the winter months), and all soldiers were required to wear a yellow reflective PT belt if out during the hours of darkness. A couple of my guys and I had just walked out of the mess hall when we were stopped by this pair of SGMs (National Guard. I only add that because it sometimes seems some Guard folks have a need to verify their importance on the battlefield). They started to give my guys a ration of shit about why they were not wearing the lifesaving reflective PT belts. I had

had about enough of them, so I stepped in and told them we had no belts (probably not true) but would be sure and wear them when we procured them. Anyone who has been around me more than a day knows I usually have a toothpick in my mouth just by habit. The SGMs looked me over and said something to the effect that I should not have a toothpick in my mouth either. Well, that was the end of my tolerance level for these two, so I said, "You have got to be fucking shittin' me. Here in a combat zone, and you can't come up with something better than that to fuck with someone about?" and I walked away before it got really ugly. I was pissed. My guys were amused, to say the least. Still hear about that incident occasionally.

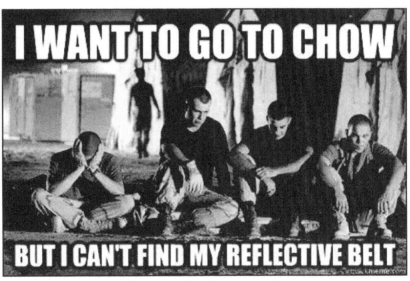

How fucking stupid is this in a combat zone?

At Kandahar with offending toothpick.

The big distractor at Kandahar was the "Shit Pond." Without a doubt the most foul-smelling sewer in the world. Period. Absolutely fucking disgusting. At times you could taste the shit; it was so bad and not a damn thing could be done about it. The airfield had grown around the sewer pond, and it had become a stinking Shit Pond that seeped into your very clothing. I can only guess that no Head Shed (High Ranking) personnel lived near enough to do anything about it. Ask anyone who ever spent any time at Kandahar, and they will tell you just how disgusting the Shit Pond was. Even got its own Facebook page, "The Poo Pond." Returned to Campbell 6 February.

The Shit Pond at Kandahar. (The Biohazard signs are real) Just looking at this picture makes me smell shit.

The Shit Pond signage was hilarious.

Gotta give a shoutout to the Navy Seabees. They built many buildings and rooms for us in Iraq and Afghanistan. They reminded me of the Disney dwarves as they showed up each morning and went immediately to work, worked all day, then packed up their shit and went back to their compound. Repeat until the job was finished. Never heard a gripe, and their work was excellent. I had never worked with Seabees before. I was impressed.

We were housed overnight at Ramstein Airbase in Germany on both the inbound and outbound portions of the rotation. We stayed in what we nicknamed the "Prison Camp." No one was allowed out of the camp. They had bunks, food, and phones available, and computers with a link to communicate with home, so it was not too bad. Just kind of a pisser to be treated like a criminal, locked in and controlled, not to be trusted among the troops assigned to Ramstein. It should be mentioned that US troops were allowed no alcohol. None. Period. Not to say alcohol was not available, just not legally. I was always an "Army of One," meaning I was the only MTP on site, so I was on-call 24 hours a day. Alcohol was not an option for me at all. The Brits and Germans had plenty of alcohol; they do not go to war without alcohol. Good plan.

Three days at BGAD and 11 days at Ft. Bragg, North Carolina, in April doing something.

25 May departed en route to Iraq. 25 June, returned to Ft. Campbell. As a note, our rotations were normally around 30 to 40 days, depending on the availability of Airforce transport. Our helicopters needed to return to Ft. Campbell about every 90 days for maintenance we could not perform in-country, so that required a monthly rotator to swap out aircraft to support a workable maintenance flow. Worked out great for us, allowing us to serve short rotations.

Deployed 3 August for Afghanistan, this time via Mazar i Sharif Airfield, or "Mez" as we called it, en route to Kunduz. (There was a great German mess hall at Mez). Caught a ride on one of our MH-47s to Kunduz. We now had a permanent footprint there based on target availability. The living conditions were good. I could cover my entire working, eating, latrine, and living area within about a 500-meter radius. Chow was excellent (for a mess hall). Conducted an NVG MTP eval while I was there. We made our first approach to what looked like a paved road outside the compound. Turned out it was a dirt road, and we totally browned out at around 50 feet. We were loaded to the maximum with weapons, bullets, fuel, and rockets, so had no power available to climb out of the dust cloud. Fortunately, the guy I was giving the eval to was quite proficient at brownout landings, and we managed to land on the road with no issues. But had to sit there for some time to burn off enough fuel to allow some leeway with power since the takeoff would be an instrument takeoff in the dust cloud. Again, my co-pilot made the takeoff with no issues. Returned to Campbell 4 September.

11 thru 15 September at Virginia Beach, Virginia.

20 thru 22 September at BGAD.

6 October deployed to Afghanistan, not sure if to Kandahar or Kunduz. Returned to Campbell 5 November.

4 thru 6 January 2011 at BGAD.

31 January to Kandahar. During this rotation, while on a target, two shitheads (Bad Guys) slipped off the target (they were called "squirters") and managed to climb a hill nearby. The AHs' on target could not climb up after them due to not having the power to effectively operate that high (about 8,000 feet). An AC-130 (armed with an array of weapons) was called in to service the targets on

the hill and I guess those guys had not gotten to engage any targets for a while. They obliterated that hilltop with everything they had. Nothing could have survived.

AC-130--just badass

The Rangers requested to be released off-target but were denied; the Head Shed (Headquarters) at Bagram wanted to find the Bad Guys (or what was left of them) to search for intelligence. I certainly felt sorry for the Rangers, knowing they had to hump up and back down that hill. By now, it was nearing daylight, so it would be a daylight extraction making it even worse. Questionable decisions by leaders were not common but sometimes happened when those making the decisions were hundreds of miles away from the target. There were some ridiculous rules of engagement in place that sometimes prevented our guys from effectively conducting missions. It usually started with a "call out" on a bullhorn, stating something to the effect of "you better come out" in Farsi (the local lingo). If that got no reaction, the next step would be a couple of "flash bangs" near a door. If that got nothing, then they would breach the door and conduct an assault accompanied by a "working dog.." Shitheads hated the dogs. Most of them would rather be shot than bitten by a dog. "Stages of escalation" was the technical name for the nightly drill. Remember, our guys conducted operations nearly every night. Also, instead of going to "the X" (a designated landing spot at or very near the target), they started doing "offset" insertions, sometimes requiring the Rangers to hump a mile or more to the target. Designed to not alert the Bad Guys to your arrival, but they usually knew you were coming through their network of communication. The Bad Guys are not stupid by any means. Returned to Campbell 5 March.

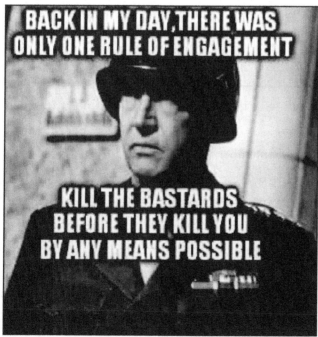

George had it right; keep it simple.

4 May deployed to Kandahar. Departed on 23 May on Emergency Leave to attend the funeral of Pam's stepfather. What a pain in the ass. Caught a C-17 to Kuwait, then a commercial flight to the US. I sat next to a mother with a baby on that commercial flight. Thank God they served free whisky. Knocked myself out for most of the flight.

Gone about a week to Ft. Lewis, Washington, in June.

7 August, deployed to Ft. Benning, Georgia, for what should have been a routine training mission support. Day one of training, an AH crashed during gunnery, killing both pilots. We had just completed the range brief for the training and flew out to the FARP, where the Little Birds armed for the range. Got the call shortly after takeoff that one of them had crashed. Bad day. Went to the crash site to set security until the Rangers took over. Waited a day until the Accident Investigation Team arrived from the Safety Center at Ft. Rucker. Returned to Ft. Campbell 10 August minus two more friends.

22 thru 28 August to Reno, Nevada. Stayed in a casino hotel in Reno, but with the hours we worked did not see or do much of anything there.

7 thru 16 September at Virginia Beach, Virginia.

17 October deployed for my last rotation to Iraq. The US was pulling out of Iraq, so it was kind of a worthless rotation. Not any targets of any significance. Spent the first three weeks or so in Talil, an airfield in the middle of nowhere Iraq. Remembered flying over it during the First Gulf War, and it was bombed to hell. It had been repaired since, and I had a hootch with my own room, shower, and, get this, my own bathroom! Plus access to the internet in my room. Unbelievable. Went to the range with the guys to shoot up most of

the ammo on hand. The range was just a spot in the desert. It was so dark that it was mostly a guess where the sky ended and the desert began. Living conditions were too good to be true for long, since on the 9th of November, we deployed to Taji Airfield near Bagdad. On the flight there, we flew over one of Saddam's palaces that had been under construction before the war. Huge complex with no lights at all; in fact, much of Bagdad still had no power at night. Kinda spooky. Returned to Ft. Campbell 17 November.

Talil, Iraq. Me front row kneeling first from left.

12 thru 17 December at Ft. Bragg, North Carolina, for something.

It came time to renew my security clearance, done every ten years or so. Since being assigned to the 160th, I have always had a TS/SCI (Top Secret, Secret Compartmentalized Information) clearance. This type of clearance was handy when you were dealing with "Need to Know" types of information. This time when I sat down with the security lady for the interview part of the clearance, she asked about a ticket I had received in 1972 for "drinking a Falls City beer on a two-lane highway." I thought, "What the fuck?! That has been in my records since I enlisted in 1975." I asked the lady what the issue was, and she replied, "You pleaded guilty and paid a 29-dollar fine." I was 16 years old, for fuck's sake. Told her I really had no choice and could not remember where I came up with the 29 dollars, and it was not on a highway but behind the local hangout where all the kids hung out. Happens that particular state cop had it in for my brothers and me for some reason (the guy was not right in the head and was later fired). Reminded her this had been in my records since 1975 and asked why it was important now. She finally let it go.

Let the record show: my enlistment record from 1975.

3 January 2012, deployed to Kandahar. We deployed to Bagram during this rotation. This was the second time I had deployed to Bagram, both to provide extra security for a POTUS (President of the US) visit. Ended up a snowstorm prevented POTUS from coming,

so it was a wasted trip. POTUS movement with all of the entourage that came with him required most of the Air Force assets in the country, so for our normal rotation, the rotator was delayed. Not the first time the rotator was delayed for POTUS trips to Afghanistan or Iraq. 10 February, returned to Ft Campbell.

2 April deployed to Kandahar. Had a new MTP with me on this rotation, so spent some time with him getting him up to speed on operations at Kandahar and the reality of conducting test flights in an AH helicopter fully armed and at maximum gross weight. Not like the generic test flights at Campbell. Returned to Campbell on a 2nd Battalion Rotator. New experience sleeping under a Chinook on the C-17.

I have not described the actual Rotator flights. Prior to departure from Campbell, we were issued two sleeping aids to get one through a ten-plus hour flight to Germany, then another ten hours to Afghanistan or Iraq. The usual routine was to take off, wait until the C-17 reached cruising altitude, then hit your pill, get in your fart sack (sleeping bag, which was laid out in a location claimed prior to takeoff), and sleep for the next ten hours. Depending on the Air Force crew, they usually let you sleep during the air-to-air (AR) refueling. Had one crew that ran cargo straps over us just to cover their ass. It could get a little rough sometimes during the AR from turbulence. Landings sometimes were a trip, again depending on the crew and the security situation at and around the arrival airfield. They would sometimes make combat approaches, which amounted to a descending circle at maximum descent rate, making for a fun approach. Think you could have tossed an apple into the air, and it would have floated. Sometimes the Air Force would carry their own security personnel to secure the aircraft while it was on the ground at some airfields that were deemed "not secure." This was hilarious to us, who got off the aircraft and lived at those airfields. We called them the "Ninja Force." They mostly got off the aircraft and ended up in positions pointing their weapons at each other and us.

USAF *Deployed 3 months to Qatar, I'm a combat veteran!

Army "Qatar is where we take R&R"

Had to get in one more jab at the Air Force.

10 thru 13 July at BGAD.

10 September deployed to Kandahar. I think it was this rotation when we got together with the German unit at Kandahar to qualify with their weapons to earn the German Marksmanship award, the "Schutzenschnur." It was quite fun as it was conducted with a sort of wink since we were also getting them qualified with our M-4 rifles and M-9 pistols. Their rifle had only day optical sights, which

seemed a little strange (How do you fight at night?) Still was fun to shoot their weapons. As an officer, I am not allowed to wear the award (not sure why), but it is still cool to have. 21 October, returned to Campbell.

3 January 2013, deployed to Kandahar. If it seems I usually had the January rotations, it was true. Someone always covered the Christmas rotations, which I really appreciated. I was always deployed for the Super Bowl games. I think that was why I usually had Christmas at home. Do not give a rat's ass about football, so it worked out. During these winter rotations, we went to work in the dark and usually went to bed in the dark. On some rotations, I would never see the sun. I think it was this rotation when I was privileged to watch an MLRS (Multiple Launch Rocket System) launch an attack on a target. It was totally impressive. The Little Birds had just landed, and the guys said they were shutting down the airfield for an MLRS launch. They must have launched about 80 rockets. Would not have wanted to be on the receiving end of that attack. Being at night, it was doubly impressive watching the rockets disappear over the horizon. 8 February, returned to Campbell.

1 thru 5 April to Ft. Lewis, Washington.

6 thru 11 May to Virginia Beach, Virginia.

10 thru 15 June to Salina, Kansas.

23 thru 27 September to Virginia Beach, Virginia.

21 thru 30 October to Savannah, Georgia.

7 January 2014 to Kandahar. 6 February, returned to Campbell.

23 thru 30 March to Ft. Lauderdale, Florida. Good trip. we worked with the Ft. Lauderdale SWAT folks quite a bit. Good people.

7 thru 11 April, I attended an Army mandated training for pending retirees called ACAP (Army Career and Alumni Program). It was an ok program meant to help prepare retirees for transition to civilian life. Much better than the "no training program" I received prior to my retirement in 1998.

10 thru 16 May at Virginia Beach, Virginia. This was my last deployment CONUS with the unit.

2 June deployed to Kandahar. My last Kandahar deployment. Had another new MTP with me, so trained him in the ways of Kandahar, then got on a 2nd Battalion rotator once again to leave early. Returned to Campbell 23 June.

All the RLOs (Real Live Officers, as we called them) and all Warrant Officers assigned to the 160th are volunteers. Many of our enlisted soldiers are volunteers, but some are assigned by DA. Let me say this about the current crop of soldiers. They are as valiant and deadly on the battlefield as the soldiers of past wars. They have different toys, likes, and ideas, but never doubt that they are trained, equipped, and ready to violently execute any mission, anywhere, anytime, + or − 30 seconds. It takes all of the different players to make that happen, so never underestimate the importance of any soldier to the mission based on their position on the battlefield. I worked with soldiers who were not born when I entered the Army. It was a great honor to serve with them. Just needed to be said.

And while I'm at it, let me say that I never found a soldier's race, religion, or sexual orientation to affect their performance. Bullets do not discriminate. We all bleed red on the battlefield.

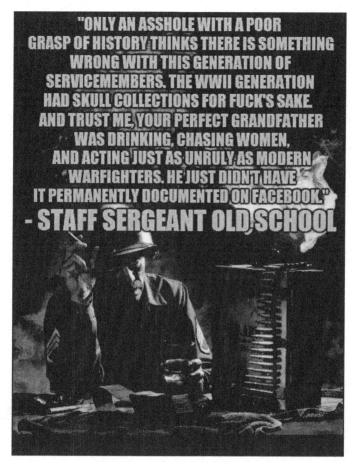

"ONLY AN ASSHOLE WITH A POOR GRASP OF HISTORY THINKS THERE IS SOMETHING WRONG WITH THIS GENERATION OF SERVICEMEMBERS. THE WWII GENERATION HAD SKULL COLLECTIONS FOR FUCK'S SAKE. AND TRUST ME, YOUR PERFECT GRANDFATHER WAS DRINKING, CHASING WOMEN, AND ACTING JUST AS UNRULY AS MODERN WARFIGHTERS. HE JUST DIDN'T HAVE IT PERMANENTLY DOCUMENTED ON FACEBOOK."
- STAFF SERGEANT OLD SCHOOL

Like I said

I was known as the "Grumpy Old Man," which was my call sign, "Grumpy." It was not that I was particularly grumpy (at least, I didn't think so); I just did not tolerate incompetence. I was responsible for several soldiers being "re-assigned" for performing poorly as a mechanic or inspector. The young soldiers hated to see me coming to preflight since it usually resulted in more work for them correcting faults I found with the aircraft. Tough shit.

Aviation has no place for anything but total dedication to the job at hand. Always seek perfection. Anything less equals failure and loss of aircraft and personnel.

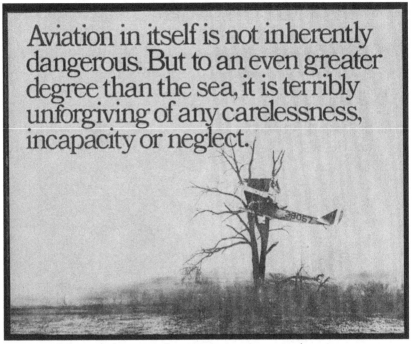

Aviation in itself is not inherently dangerous. But to an even greater degree than the sea, it is terribly unforgiving of any carelessness, incapacity or neglect.

I do not tolerate carelessness, incapacity, or neglect…ever.

Flying has been my therapy. I could never believe I was being paid to fly. In the cockpit, nothing else mattered to me but operating the helicopter. The world's worries can wait…fly the helicopter. Always fly the damn helicopter. You owe it to yourself, your passengers, your family, and the taxpayer (which I am also) to land the aircraft the same as it was when you took off. Enough ranting.

29 July, I made my last flight as an Army Aviator. Flew down to the Shelbyville, Tennessee, airfield and met my daughter and grandkids there. Flew NVGs back to Campbell. The end of my Army Aviator career...again.

Me and Rick prior to strapping in for my last flight as an Army Aviator.

Spent August thru November doing all the shit you have to do to retire. I had gone to the flight surgeon a few months prior to my last flight and asked him to set me up with all the appointments with the various entities to get documentation of all my ailments so I could hopefully get some disability from the VA this retirement (none for my first retirement). If it is not documented on paper, it did not happen, according to the VA. He hooked me up. I had a shitload of appointments. Had a thick packet of documentation of my ailments to present to my VA guy to send forward to the VA Folks in the sky or wherever those mythical persons resided.

Had an appointment with CIF to turn in all my equipment again. I left with about half the shit I packed into CIF. Still have a shit ton of stuff. Not sure how that happened.

Threw myself a retirement party in October. Good night with a lot of good friends. During this occasion, Pam was presented the "Our Lady of Loretto Medal" to recognize her many years of service to Army Aviation. This is a high honor only awarded to a deserving few, presented by the Army Aviation Association of America. She certainly deserved it.

2014 retirement party; the rocking chair a retirement gift.

I feel I have included too many boring accounts of deployment after deployment, but many of the guys I served with completed countless and longer deployments over many more years than myself. My deployments are indeed trivial compared to many.

Retired for the second time on 29 November 2014. (Pam's birthday, so she got a little extra present that year.) 30 years 1 month 24 days.

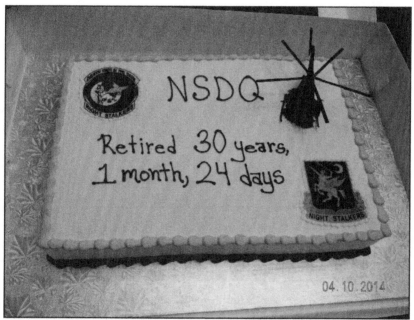

Retirement cake Pam had made for my second retirement

My wife says I have used the word "fuck" too much in this story. Truth is, I have watered the use down quite a bit from the real world. To GIs of any service, male or female, "fuck" is used as a verb, adverb, adjective, noun, pronoun, etc. It can be proceeded by any number of descriptive words to add to the meaning or be followed by any number of words to do the same. Not going to apologize for my use of the word. Would be like watching the movie *Patton* with Old George never uttering a curse word. Just wouldn't be right.

Well, fuck you then.

IF YOU KNOW A VETERAN

Chances are that he or she seems friendly and also seems like an open book. But make no mistake, there are chapters removed due to the fact that they are not fit for public consumption.

Oh, yes!

14.

SINCE THEN...

After a few months off, I went to work back on the 160th Compound for a contractor company that wrote and published publications for the 160th aircraft. Lots of desk time at a computer. Hated it. A position became available to fly as an MTP contractor with Lockheed Martin, the current holder of the civilian aircraft maintenance contract, so, once again, I was test flying Little Birds and going on trips inside CONUS for training with SOATB (Special Operations Aviation Training Battalion). Had an issue with the Rucker Flight Surgeons being concerned with my having spent a couple of days hospitalized when I was around nine years old for a wasp sting. Really? Once again, pointed out that this had been in my medical records since 1975. And was no one concerned with the fact I had been cross-eyed for a time? I mean, what the fuck? This, too, eventually was dropped. I was happily deploying for training and test-flying once again. Also, during this time period, I had gotten my fixed-wing private pilot's license in a Piper Cherokee airplane. I really enjoyed fixed-wing flying, which was surprising, with me loving to fly helicopters. In 2017 the Flight Surgeon ran some extra blood tests for my annual flight physical because "you're an old guy." Well, turned out one of the tests was about three times what it was supposed to be, which led to a series of tests that ended with me back at Vanderbilt in the Cath lab getting a heart stint. I had been living with the "dead man walking" artery blockage. One artery was totally blocked, and my heart had bypassed it on its own (I don't understand how all that worked). The rerouted artery was 75 percent blocked and got a stint. I had no symptoms at all. The bottom line was neither the Army nor the FAA would allow me to continue flying with the totally blocked artery. I asked my heart doc if it was possible to unblock the artery, and he said it was possible. I asked him if he would have the procedure if it were him, and he said he would not. That was good enough for me. So ended my flying career. I do occasionally fly with a friend in an airplane and still enjoy it a lot.

I am now fully retired with 100 percent VA disability. It turned out to be a great decision to return to active duty as the second time I retired at the current pay scale, which was significantly higher than the 1998 pay scale (nearly twice my 1998 retirement paycheck). I collect and enjoy old cars, build models, and basically don't do much of anything other than go to endless doctors' appointments and, these days, too many funerals." Getting old ain't for sissies," as my brother Garry always said. I hope this hasn't been too terribly boring. Thanks to those of you who made it to:

The End.

Badassery at Kandahar.

Kandahar with no alcohol allowed; guess I didn't hear much.

Night Stalker Memorial on the 160th Compound at Ft. Campbell.
Names of Night Stalkers who are killed in combat or training are etched on
this marble monument. 62 names were added while I was with the unit…62!
FREEDOM IS NOT FREE! Never has been and never will be.

On the anniversary of the death of each soldier whose name is on the
memorial, friends gather to remember them
through stories and a toast to their life.

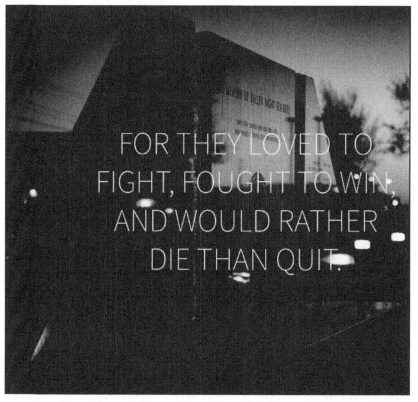

FOR THEY LOVED TO FIGHT, FOUGHT TO WIN, AND WOULD RATHER DIE THAN QUIT.

NSDQ!

Night Stalker Creed

Service in the 160th is a calling only a few will answer for the mission is constantly demanding and hard. And when the impossible has been accomplished the only reward is another mission that no one else will try. As a member of the Night Stalkers I am a tested volunteer seeking only to safeguard the honor and prestige of my country, by serving the elite Special Operations Soldiers of the United States. I pledge to maintain my body, mind and equipment in a constant state of readiness for I am a member of the fastest deployable Task Force in the world, ready to move at a moment's notice anytime, anywhere, arriving time on target plus or minus 30 seconds.

I guard my unit's mission with secrecy, for my only true ally is the night and the element of surprise. My manner is that of the Special Operations Quiet Professional, secrecy is a way of life. In battle, I eagerly meet the enemy for I volunteered to be up front where the fighting is hard. I fear no foe's ability, nor underestimate his will to fight.

The mission and my precious cargo are my concern. I will never surrender. I will never leave a fallen comrade to fall into the hands of the enemy, and under no circumstances will I ever embarrass my country.

Gallantly will I show the world and the elite forces I support that a Night Stalker is a specially selected and well trained soldier.

I serve with the memory and pride of those who have gone before me for they loved to fight, fought to win and would rather die than quit.

Night Stalkers Don't Quit!

"The Lord knows the way I take, and when He has tested me, I shall come forth as gold" JOB 23:10

My medals, rack, salad bar (worn on the left side of the uniform). One accumulates a few over 30 years.

Bronze Star Medal, Meritorious Service Medal W/2 Oak Leaf Clusters, Air Medal, Army Commendation Medal W/3 Oak Leaf Clusters, Army Achievement Medal W/2 Oak Leaf Clusters, Army Good Conduct Medal W/2 Knots, National Defense Service Medal W/1 Bronze Star, Armed Forces Expeditionary Medal, Southwest Asia Service Medal W/2 Bronze Stars, Afghanistan Campaign Medal W/2 Bronze Stars, Iraq Campaign Medal W/3 Bronze Stars, Global War On Terrorism Medal (Service), Korean Defense Service Medal, Military Outstanding Volunteer Service Medal, Army NCO Professional Development Medal W/Numeral 2, Army Service Ribbon, Overseas Service Ribbon W/Numeral 2, NATO Medal, Kuwait Liberation Medal (Saudi Arabia), Kuwait Liberation Medal (Kuwait)

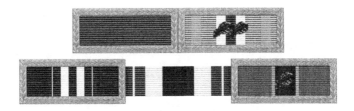

Unit Awards (right side of uniform)

Presidential Unit Citation, Joint Meritorious Unit Award W/2 Oak Leaf Clusters, Valorous Unit Award, Meritorious Unit Commendation/ USA/USAF, Army Superior Unit Award W/1 Oak Leaf Cluster

(Must be assigned to the unit at the time of the award for permanent wear. All of mine were with the 160th, other than the Army Superior Unit Award, with one from the 268th AHB and one from JTF Bravo)

In case you were wondering…

Bronze Service Star is also known as Campaign or Battle Stars, bronze service stars are worn on service ribbons to denote an additional award of a medal or to indicate participation in a designated campaign.

An Oak Leaf Cluster is a common device that is placed on military awards and decorations to denote those who have received more than one bestowal of a particular decoration. The number of Oak Leaf Clusters typically indicates the second and subsequent award of the decoration.

Numeral Devices are Arabic numerals attached to certain ribbons and medals to denote multiple decorations of the same award. These devices are unique in that the U.S. Army is the only military branch to use numerals.

And also, yes, those pieces of ribbon do mean something to us.

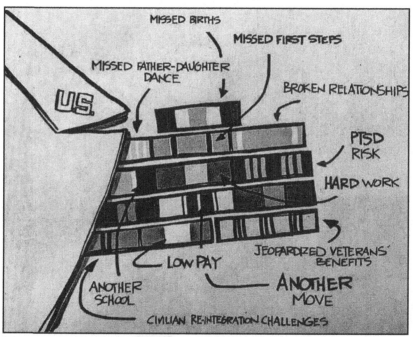

Seemed more like this sometimes for most of us.

Badges earned:

Master Army Aviator badge.

Air Assault badge.

Combat Service Identification badges and Drill Sergeant Identification badge.

The first three are 101st, 160th, and Special Operations Command Combat Service Identification Badges (badges worn on the right pocket to denote units assigned to during combat tours). The 101st for Desert Storm, the 160th for Enduring Freedom, and the SOCOM for Iraqi Freedom and Enduring Freedom. The 160th changed to the current patch during my last couple of rotations in Afghanistan. Only one badge may be worn at a time, so I usually go with the 160th badge. The fourth is my Drill Sergeant badge (AKA "The Pumpkin").

Aircraft Qualifications:
Army:
TH-55A, UH-1H, OH-58A/C, UH-60A, MH-60A/ L/ K/, MH/AH-6C/ G/ N/ J/ M
Civilian:
Piper Cherokee PA 28

Total Flight Hours: 7296
Combat: 291
NVG: 800+
Various Simulators: 300+

Countries deployed to:
West Germany (it was West Germany when I was there)
South Korea
Honduras
Saudi Arabia
Iraq

Kuwait

Afghanistan

Panama

Ecuador

Israel

Cuba (Guantanamo Bay)

Puerto Rico

Okinawa (Japan)

Dominican Republic

Countries I have drunk a beer in (It's our criteria for if one can claim having been there:

Great Britain

Spain

Hawaii (seemed like another country)

Holland

I threw this in for the amusement of any old soldiers reading this. Only they will really get it. For non-old soldiers, read it anyhow, even if you don't get it; it's how it really was. An explanation of some of the acronyms and lingo follows number 35.

HOW TO TELL YOU'RE AN OLD SOLDIER:

1. You remember spending hours in MOPP4 and doing M256 kits.

2. When the M18 Claymore Mine and M72 LAW were part of CTT.

3. You remember when ARTEPs were 36 hours and you had fun.

4. You know what a CEOI is, and you can encrypt grids.

5. You remember Bn Cmdrs. who drank, swore, and mentored.

6. You remember Bn Cmdrs. who were ruthless about tactics but didn't give a crap about admin bullshit.

7. You remember when 2LTs and CPLs demanded respect from PFCs and got it.

8. You remember how to report for pay and what a pay line was.

9. You remember beer machines in the barracks/dayroom.

10. When there used to be enlisted, NCO and Officer Clubs.

11. What an alert was.

12. When Sergeants ran the Army.

13. Only elite forces wore a beret.

14. When Saturday was for inspections and Monday through Friday was for training.

15. You remember when an Article-15 did not end your career.

16. You know what Blood Stripes are.

17. You remember what the "Colonel's Orderly" was.

18. Connie Rod had big boobs.

19. You were allowed two beers for lunch.

20. You knew the difference between a "Radboro" and a "Marlboro"

21. You remember Flippies at Graf or Hohenfels.

22. Two Words: Cunt Cap.

23. You can tell the story about accidentally entering the 1K zone.

24. When seeing someone with an ARCOM was a total rarity.

25. You remember the SQT.

26. You remember the ranks Spec 5,6, and 7.

27. You remember organization days with beer (and you WILL have fun)

28. You used brasso and kiwi daily.

29. You fixed the heater in your M60A1 routinely, becoming a Master Heater Repair Sergeant.

30. Night acquisitions from the PDO yard were expected.

31. You know what a "Supernumerary" is and tried hard to get it.

32. You remember John Wayne bars and cigarettes in C-Rats.

33. You know what a P-38 is.

34. You remember dehydrated meat patties and fruit in MREs.

35. And finally, you remember when a dollar was worth almost four Deutsche Marks.

Let me "splains it" for you non-old soldiers.

#1. MOPP4 = Mission Oriented Protective Posture. There were four levels of increasing layers of NBC (Nuclear, Biological, and Chemical) protective gear worn with four being the highest. MOPP4 nearly rendered one useless. M256 kits were used to detect blood, blister, and nerve agents.

Soldiers in MOPP 4 (really sucked in hot weather, and flying with all that shit on double sucked)

#2. The M18 Claymore mine is a wicked-ass antipersonnel mine filled with ball bearings. It hilariously has "Front Towards Enemy" on the front to make sure you don't fuck yourself up. The M72 LAW is a Light Anti-Tank Weapon—a bazooka. During the Vietnam War, some of these tended to blow up when they were extended for use. The Vietnam vets I worked with would not fire one, so I always got to shoot the range demo LAW. Couldn't hit shit with it. CTT is Common Task Training, something all soldiers were required to know and do.

M18 Claymore Anti-personnel mine

M72 LAW (extended)

#3. ARTEP—Army Training and Evaluation Program, required once a year by all Army units. Mostly a pain in the ass due to Commanders wanting to get their ticket punched.

#4. CEOI—Communications-Electronics Operating Instructions. A classified booklet that allowed one to encrypt/decrypt messages. I remember burning used pages, which had to be witnessed and documented.

#11. Most units have practice alerts at least once a month. This usually consists of a 2 AM phone call, beeper buzz, or some other form of contact (they used a siren at LaGuardia Airfield in Korea). This was followed by drawing of weapons, preflight, and whatever other go-to-war preparations needed to be completed. The alert period could last from a couple of hours to a couple of days.

#15. Article-15. This is a form of punishment doled out for most minor offenses, usually forfeiting some pay along with extra duty and restriction to the barracks. Nowadays nearly career-ending; back in the day not really a big deal.

#16. Blood Stripes resulted from the tradition of smacking a newly earned rank pin into your collar. Shit hurt and bled, thus "Blood Stripes." Since discontinued. Probably for the better.

#17. Colonel's Orderly was just a nice term for the Colonel's bitch boy.

#18. Connie Rodd was a cartoon character hosting the *PS Magazine*, officially known as *The Preventive Maintenance Monthly*, and, well, she had big boobs. Always reminded me of "Hot Lips" from *MASH*. Not politically correct these days.

Connie Rodd

#20. Radboro was a nickname for a German version of a cigarette that was just nasty. Germans loved American cigarettes, making them prime bartering fodder.

#21. Flippies was German beer in bottles with the cap attached to the bottle by a hinge. They were refillable, so were kept and traded in for full ones.

#22. Cunt Cap, officially known as the Army Garrison Cap. Just use your imagination a little.

Pic of the cunt cap I wore with dress greens while assigned to the 101st.

#23. Ahh, the 1K Zone. Remember my story?

#24. ARCOM—Army Commendation Medal. It was rare indeed to see medals of any kind on any soldier other than the Vietnam Vets.

#25. SQT—Skill Qualification Test. A series of tests, administered to all soldiers once a year evaluating numerous skills required by your MOS (Military Occupational Specialty). A high score looked good for promotion boards, so rampant cheating became the norm.

#26. Specialist 5, 6 and even 7 ranks were used to progress soldiers in jobs so that they could become experts at their jobs without being NCOs. Needed again. Now it's move up or move out.

#30. PDO yard—Property Disposal Yard. The place where all used, broken, and outdated equipment went for storage and later to be sold at auction. GIs would often raid the yard to obtain parts that would sometimes take weeks to get through the "system." Sometimes legally and sometimes not.

#31. Supernumerary. The top soldier from an in-ranks guard duty inspection. That soldier was released from guard duty. I never made Supernumerary. I always had stained uniforms.

#32. Field rations, C-Rats, or C- Rations. John Wayne bars are round, flat chocolate bars sometimes included as dessert. Surprisingly good. The pound cake and peaches were really good. A four-pack of random-brand cigarettes was included. They removed the cigarettes in 1972 but issued them until they were exhausted, so they had them until around 1976. It was a real challenge to wipe your ass with that tiny bit of shit paper.

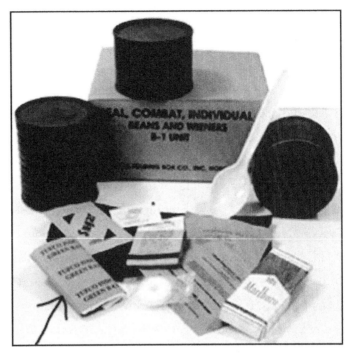

C Rats. arrow points to C-Rat shit paper

#33. P-38 = A can opener included with all C-Rats. All GIs carried a P-38, usually with dog tags or on a keychain.

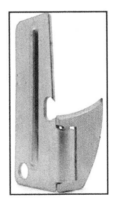

P-38

#34. MRE—Meal, Ready to Eat, the replacement for C-Rats. Not as good as C-Rats in my book, but I did not need a P-38 to open cans.

#35. Deutsche Marks were the German currency until being replaced by the Euro in 2002. The D-mark rate varied from day to day, so one closely watched the rate of exchange to decide when to pay rent and other bills if living in the economy. I never saw a four-D-mark rate while there; it stayed around 1.60 D-marks per dollar.

Art by
Capt Ed Cooke

Helicopter Pilots Are Different

"The thing is, helicopters are different from planes. An airplane by its nature wants to fly, and if not interfered with too strongly by unusual events or by a deliberately incompetent pilot, it will fly. A helicopter does not want to fly. It is maintained in the air by a variety of forces and controls working in opposition to each other, and if there is any disturbance in this delicate balance the helicopter stops flying, immediately and disastrously.

"There is no such thing as a gliding helicopter.

"This is why being a helicopter pilot is so different from being an airplane pilot, and why, in general, airplane pilots are open, clear-eyed, bouyant extroverts, and helicopter pilots are brooders, introspective anticipators of trouble. They know if something bad has not happened, it is about to."

—*Harry Reasoner*

Yes, we are.

Mostly true

"I DRINK AND I KNOW THINGS"

TURNS OUT TYRION IS A WARRANT OFFICER

Absolutely true

and the truth is that
all veterans pay with
their lives.
some pay all at once,
while others pay
over a lifetime.

Also true

I submitted the following article to the 1/160th Safety Officer for inclusion in their monthly Safety Letter. It was rejected for including too many obscenities, which was fucking hilarious.

I should also explain some of the content. Army aviation accidents are classified by the Army from A to E based on the cost of the mishap. A fatality accident is always a Class A. A PRAM is a Preliminary Report of Aircraft Mishap used for rapid reporting of minor incidents. The SHOC pad is a training area on the Ft. Campbell Reservation used exclusively by the 160th. EENT is End of Evening Nautical Twilight, about 30 minutes after official sunset. An APART (Annual Proficiency and Readiness Test) is a period of time designated by an Aviators birth month when an aircraft check ride, flight physical, and other requirements are due. OGE is an out-of-ground effect hover, a maneuver used to gauge a helicopter's power availability and controllability. A stall check is a test flight maneuver that tries to induce or duplicate an engine stall. It is a violent maneuver even when performed by seasoned test pilots. Veterans call all such stories as this and anything else about one's military experiences "War Stories."

War Story

We always hear about the Class A, B, or C accidents. Class Es usually get a PRAM written up and are forgotten. It has been said that most Class Es were not Class As only by good judgment, superior pilot skills, or plain good luck. I agree and so begins this War Story.

I was to conduct an annual APART day/NVG check ride. All pre-flight planning, the pre-flight, and oral examination had gone well. We strapped in, cranked, and departed to SHOC pad to conduct the day portion of the APART. All-day maneuvers were completed without incident. We waited until EENT and goggled up for the NVG part of the APART. After one hour of NVG flight, we were repositioning for an OGE hover check. At a three-foot forward hover, we heard a loud bang, and the aircraft yawed. I don't remember who was actually flying, but by the time I said, "What the fuck was that!" We had landed. Both of us being maintenance test pilots, we naturally began to troubleshoot the problem or perceived problem. "Compressor stall?" ... "Didn't feel like it." ..." Wanta try a stall check?" ...." Naw" ..." Think somethin' hit the tail rotor?" ...." Could have" ..." Let's shut down and check it out" (the throttle was at idle now)." Maybe we should reposition over by the road so if it's broken, they can get to it with the trailer easier" (by now I was beginning to roll the throttle back up because it made sense to move the aircraft over by the road) ..." Naw, let's shut the bitch down and take a look" .... (At which time I rolled the throttle back to idle.)

We shut down and discovered that the tail rotor would turn about 90 degrees without any movement of the main rotor. Being the superbly trained, steely-eyed maintenance test pilots that we were, we immediately recognized this as a bad thing. Further inspection revealed that the forward tail rotor driveshaft flex coupling had failed. Fortunately, the fail-safe feature I had always heard about but really didn't believe would work, worked.

I'm not really sure why I didn't roll the throttle back up to reposition the aircraft....and why we didn't try a stall check or two. Maybe the fail-safe feature would have held together for the rest of the flight.... or not.

The moral of the story is...if you think there's a problem, there probably is. Land the dam thing and shut it down. You could be a gnat's ass away from a Class A.

CW4 Barker F 1/160 SOAR Safety Officer

Article my brother Garry wrote chronicling my Black Hawk helicopter flight to Flemingsburg to salute my Dad

Stories are a tribute to family
Garry Barker
Columnist

When my short story "Kentucky Waltz" appeared in the summer issue of Berea College's Appalachian Heritage magazine, it was with permission from the real-life helicopter pilot who made an unauthorized trip over to Flemingsburg.

He's retired now from the U.S. Army and relatively safe from a court martial.

Sharyn McCrumb wrote the episode into her Rosewood Casket novel but cut the passage when a retired general told her she'd get somebody court-martialed if she printed the story. It was too true, he said, to be fiction, and somebody somewhere would track down the facts.

After about eight years, we figured we'd declassify the information. When our father was dying in Flemingsburg, the youngest brother, Jon, brought a U.S. Army helicopter into town and dropped down to window level for a final salute to the WW II veteran who was watching, and in the process scared the daylights out of every dog, cat, calf and coyote in his path.

Not very long-ago Jon flew out over our place, and circled low, but I mistook him for a "pot chopper," the airborne marijuana sniffers of the Kentucky National Guard. As I e-mailed Jon later, I did not shoot at him, but can't vouch for all the neighbors. A low flying camouflaged gunship, in Eastern Kentucky, is usually not a friendly sign.

Jon is now a civilian test pilot, flying the Army's helicopters, doing much the same job except not flying actual combat missions. He did his share of that, all over the world, with the 101st Airborne and then with the elite 160th Special Operations Aviation Regiment.

Jon's most memorable flight, to me, will always be the one to the house on High Street, where he delighted my parents despite the racket and the roar he brought down with him.

My version of the flight is mostly fiction. I rigged the chopper up with speakers to play Bluegrass music, sounds my brother Jon would not allow near him, and tossed in lots of irrelevant details. I am not, after all, one to let facts stand in the way of a good tale.

So grab you a copy of the summer 2002 Appalachian Heritage and share the waltz across Kentucky in a Blackhawk helicopter.

I think you'll be glad you did.

Up close and personal in an MH-6M… just because I could.

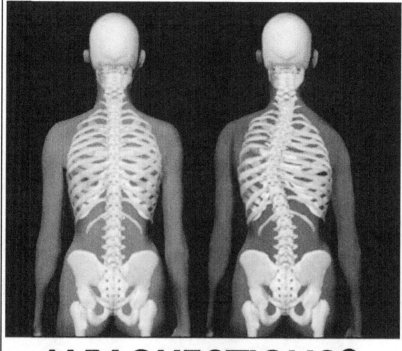

THIS IS YOUR BACK. **THIS IS YOUR BACK AFTER YEARS IN A HELICOPTER.**

ANY QUESTIONS?

Exactly! A big part of why I was awarded 100 percent permanent disability by the VA. along with my knees, arthritis, hearing, etc.

Self- explanatory

Dave Barry article about his flight in a helicopter. Had to include it...too realistic and funny not to.

Whirlybirdbrain

TODAY'S AVIATION TOPIC IS: "HOW to fly a helicopter." Although flying a helicopter may seem very difficult, the truth is that if you can drive a car, you can, with just a few minutes of instruction, take the controls of one of these amazing machines. Of course you would immediately crash and die. This is why you need to remember:

RULE 1 OF HELICOPTER PILOTING: Always have somebody sitting right next to you who actually knows how to fly a helicopter and can snatch the controls away from you.

Because the truth is that helicopters are nothing at all like cars. Cars work because of basic scientific principles that everybody understands, such as internal combustion and parallel parking. Whereas scientists still have no idea what holds helicopters up. "Whatever it is, it could stop at any moment," is their current feeling. This leads us to:

RULE 2 OF HELICOPTER PILOTING: Maybe you should forget the entire thing.

This was what I was thinking on a recent Saturday morning as I stood outside a small airport where I was about to take my first helicopter lesson. This was not my idea. This was the idea of Pam Gallina-Raissiguier, a pilot who flies radio reporters during rush hour.

Pam is active in an international organization of women helicopter pilots called—Gloria Steinem, avert your eyes—the "Whirly Girls." She thought it would be a great idea for me to take a helicopter lesson.

I began having severe doubts when I saw Pam's helicopter. This was a small helicopter. It looked like it should have a little slot where you insert quarters to make it go up and down. Also, it had no doors. As a Frequent Flyer, I know for a fact that all the leading U.S. airlines, despite being bankrupt, maintain a strict safety policy of having doors on their aircraft.

"Don't we need a larger helicopter?" I asked Pam. "With doors?"

"Get in," said Pam.

You don't defy a direct order from a Whirly Girl.

Now we're in the helicopter, and Pam is explaining the controls to me over the headset. Then suddenly she is moving a control thing and WHOOAAA we are off the ground, hovering, and now WHOOOOAAAAAA we are shooting up in the air, and there are still no doors on this particular helicopter.

Now Pam is giving me the main control thing.

RULE 3 OF HELICOPTER PILOTING: If anybody tries to give you the main control thing, refuse to take it.

Pam says: "You don't need hardly any pressure to . . ."

AIEEEEEEEEEEEEEE!

"That was too much pressure," Pam says.

Now I am flying the helicopter. I AM FLYING THE HELICOPTER. I am flying it by not moving a single body part, for fear of jiggling the control thing. I look like the Lincoln Memorial statue of Abraham Lincoln, only more rigid.

"Make a right turn," Pam is saying.

I gingerly move the control thing one zillionth of an inch to the right and the helicopter LEANS OVER TOWARD MY

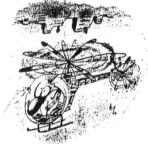

SIDE AND THERE IS STILL NO DOOR HERE. I instantly move the thing one zillionth of an inch back.

"I'm not turning right," I inform Pam.

"What?" she says.

"Only left turns," I tell her. When you've been flying helicopters as long as I have, you know your limits.

After a while it becomes clear to Pam that if she continues to allow the Lincoln statue to pilot the helicopter, we are going to wind up flying in a straight line until we run out of fuel, possibly over Antarctica, so she takes the control thing back. That is the good news. The bad news is, she's now saying something about demonstrating an "emergency procedure."

"It's for when your engine dies," Pam says. "It's called 'auto-rotation.' Do you like amusement park rides?"

I say: "No, I DOOOOOOOOOOOO . . ."

RULE 4 OF HELICOPTER PILOTING: "Auto-rotation" means "coming down out of the sky at about the same speed and aerodynamic stability as that of a forklift dropped from a bomber."

Now we're close to the ground (although my stomach is still at 500 feet), and Pam is completing my training by having me hover the helicopter.

RULE 5 OF HELICOPTER PILOTING: You can't hover the helicopter.

The idea is to hang over one spot on the ground. I am hovering over an area about the size of Australia. I am swooping around sideways and backward like a crazed bumblebee. If I were trying to rescue a person from the roof of a 100-story burning building, the person would realize that it would be safer to simply jump.

So I am very happy when we finally get back on the ground. Pam tells me I did great, and she'd be glad to take me up again. I tell her that sounds like a fun idea.

RULE 6 OF HELICOPTER PILOTING: Sometimes you have to lie. ∎

Chronology of Military Service for CW4 Jon P. Barker

1975: August 29, joined the US Army at Ft. Knox, Kentucky, as a Private E-1. Completed basic training and AIT.

1975-1978: Assigned to E Troop 2nd Squadron 6th Cavalry Brigade at Ft. Knox. Served as Tank Driver, Loader, Gunner, and Commander on a Sheridan Tank (M551A1). Completed Primary Non-Commissioned Officer Course. Promoted from Private through Sergeant E-5.

1978-1979: Assigned to A Company 4th Battalion 69th Armor, Mainz, West Germany. Served as Gunner and Commander of an M60A1 Tank. (14 months)

1979-1981: Assigned to E Company 2nd Battalion 1st Training Brigade, Ft. Knox. Served as Tank Commander/Instructor. Completed Drill Sergeant School and served two years as a Drill Sergeant. Promoted to SSG E-6.

1982: Assigned to Ft. Rucker, Alabama. Completed flight school. Completed AQCs in the TH-55A, UH-1H, and OH-58A/C helicopters. Promoted to WO1.

1983: Assigned to C Company 268th Attack Helicopter Battalion, Ft. Lewis, Washington, as an OH-58A/C Aero Scout Pilot.

1984: Promoted to CW2.

1985: Completed OH-58A/C Maintenance Test Pilot Course, Ft. Eustis, Virginia.

1986: Completed UH-60A AQC, Ft Rucker, Alabama, completed UH-60A MTP Course, Ft. Eustis, Virginia.

1987: Assigned to D Troop 4/7 Cavalry, Camp La Guardia, Uijongbu, Korea, as a UH-60A MTP and Technical Supply Officer.

(12 months) Completed Aviation Warrant Officer Advanced Course. (through correspondence)

1988: Assigned to B Company 8th Battalion, 101st Aviation Brigade Aviation Intermediate Maintenance Company (AVIM), Ft. Campbell, Kentucky, as Maintenance Platoon Leader. Completed Air Assault Course.

1989: Completed UH-1H MTP Course, Ft. Eustis, Virginia.

1989/90: Assigned to JTF Bravo, Honduras, as UH-60A/UH-1H MTP, Technical Supply Officer/Maintenance Platoon Leader. (4 months)

1990/91: Deployed to Operation Desert Shield/Desert Storm as a UH1H/UH60A MTP, Promoted to CW3. (7 months)

1991: Assigned to F Company 1st Battalion, 160th SOAR. Ft. Campbell. Completed AQC and MTP training in an A/MH-6. Completed "Green Platoon" training.

1992: Completed MH-60A/L AQC and MTP Course, completed SERE (Survival, Evasion, Resistance, and Escape (Level C), North Island NAS, San Diego, California.

1994: Completed Aviation Safety Officer Course, Ft. Rucker, Alabama.

1995: Completed MH-60K AQC and MTP Course.

1996: Completed A/MH-6 IP Course, Ft. Indiantown Gap, Pennsylvania. Promoted to CW4.

1997: Completed Warrant Officer Staff Course, Ft. Rucker, Alabama.

1998-2007, November, Retired. Hired as civilian contractor as an A/MH-6 and MH-60 MTP for the 160th SOAR.

2007: November, Returned to Active Duty, reassigned to F1/160th SOAR.

2008: May, completed first tour (rotation) in Iraq, OIF. (Operation Iraqi Freedom) December, completed second rotation OIF.

2009: June, completed third rotation OIF.

2010: February, completed first rotation in Afghanistan, OEF. (Operation Enduring Freedom)

2010: June, completed fourth rotation OIF.

2010: September, completed second rotation. November, completed third rotation OEF.

2011: March, completed fourth rotation. May, completed fifth rotation OEF.

2011: November, completed fifth (and last) rotation Iraq, OND. (Operation New Dawn)

2012: February, completed sixth rotation OEF.

2012: April, completed seventh rotation OEF.

2012: October, completed eighth rotation OEF.

2013: January, completed ninth rotation OEF.

2014: February, completed tenth rotation OEF.

2014: June, completed eleventh (and last) rotation OEF.

2014: November 29, retired for the second time.

All Army aviators sew patches on their helmet bags. Becomes a kind of chronology of a career in itself. My original flight helmet bag issued in 1982 with various patches.

Other side of my helmet bag

Various name tags. Note Standard Cockpit Brief top left. Bottom left known as "Blood Tag."

Stuff from my enlisted time. Below the dog tag is my Expert Qualification Badge for Pistol and Tank Weapons. I could also add grenade and rifle. Near the bottom right are all my enlisted ranks insignia, right to left, Private through Staff Sergeant.

More stuff. The front of the ballcap is from my Korea tour; the hat fell apart. I couldn't afford the Stetson hats many of the guys bought. The tool at the top right is used to open and close panel fasteners on helicopters, known as a "Snoopy Tool," for obvious reasons.

AH-6J with various weapons and ammunition available. Shown here are
HellFire missiles, GAU-19 .50 caliber Gatling guns, 7-shot 2.75 rocket pods,
and 7.62 mini-guns

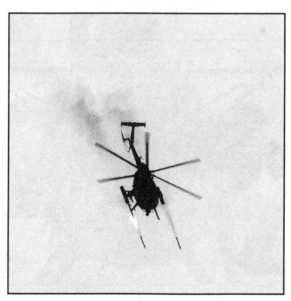

AH-6-M launching 2.75 Rockets

MH-60 loaded with "The Boys"

MH6 loaded with "The Boys"

MH-60 DAP with Hellfire missiles, 30mm chain gun, and 7.62 mini-guns.

MH60 dropping off "The Boys" to catch another ride. Could have been one my brother Bill's subs. He told me some stories.

Night Stalker Unit logo patch

It was a real dilemma for sure between rotations.

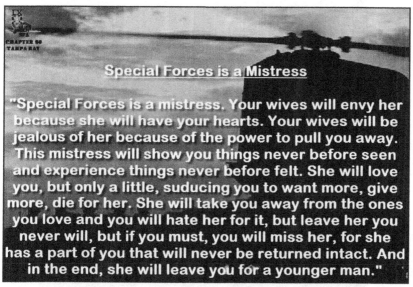

Special Forces is a Mistress

"Special Forces is a mistress. Your wives will envy her because she will have your hearts. Your wives will be jealous of her because of the power to pull you away. This mistress will show you things never before seen and experience things never before felt. She will love you, but only a little, suducing you to want more, give more, die for her. She will take you away from the ones you love and you will hate her for it, but leave her you never will, but if you must, you will miss her, for she has a part of you that will never be returned intact. And in the end, she will leave you for a younger man."

She's a bitch for sure, and in the end, it is a young man's game.

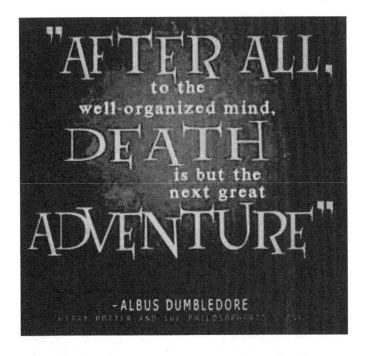

"AFTER ALL,
to the
well-organized mind,
DEATH
is but the
next great
ADVENTURE"

-ALBUS DUMBLEDORE
HARRY POTTER AND THE PHILOSOPHER'S STONE

Just because I give
you advice, It doesn't mean
I know more than you.
It just means I've done
more stupid shit.

Unknown

GOOD THINGS DON'T COME TO THOSE WHO WAIT. THEY COME TO THOSE WHO WORK THEIR ASSES OFF AND NEVER GIVE UP.

Unknown

Society can exist only on the basis that there is some amount of polished lying and that no one says exactly what he thinks --Lin Yutang

Experience is a marvelous thing that enables you to recognize a mistake when you make it again. --Franklin P. Adams

A rule that cannot be bent will certainly be broken. --Ned Arthur

If they really want to honor the soldiers, why don't they let them sit in the stands and have the people march by? --Will Rogers

Nothing can be so perfect while we possess it as it will when remembered --Oliver Wendell Holmes

Of all liars, the smoothest and most convincing is memory. --Unknown. (So true. Writing this has proved that to me.)

Life is what happens to you while you are making other plans -John Lennon

There is limited value in giving advice to folks who need food. -The Country Parson

The only man who never makes a mistake is the man who never does anything. -Theodore Roosevelt

Avoiding danger is no safer in the long run than outright exposure. Life is either a daring adventure or nothing. -Helen Keller

If the truth doesn't help, lie. -Unknown. (One of my favorites.)

The man who resolves to deal with none but the honest must leave off dealing. -Thomas Fuller

No amount of pay ever made a good soldier, a good teacher, a good artist, or a good workman. -John Ruskin

If you insist on perfection, make the first demand on yourself. -Our Daily Bread

Advice after mischief is like medicine after death. -American Saying

The way I see it, if you want the rainbow, you gotta put up with the rain. -Dolly Parton

Successful people make decisions quickly (as soon as all the facts are available) and change them slowly. Unsuccessful people make decisions very slowly and change them often and quickly. -Napoleon Hill

When Albert Wiggam, Author of Explore Your Mind," was asked if lack of ability caused most failures, he said, "No. Fear does. It defeats more people than poverty, ignorance, superstition, ill health, and lack of mental ability."

Worrying is a waste of time. It doesn't change anything. It messes with your mind and steals your happiness.

True. I only worry about things I can control. I don't think one could be a helicopter pilot if one worried about what "could" or "might" happen.

The following are excerpts from *The Notebooks of Lazarus Long* from the book *Time Enough for Love: The Lives of Lazarus Long* written by Robert A. Heinlein. Terrific book. Read it if you get a chance.

Your enemy is never a villain in his own eyes. (Remember, the Nazis wore belt buckles with "God with us" on them.)

Cheop's Law: Nothing ever gets built on schedule or within budget.

All men are created unequal.

You can have peace. Or you can have freedom. Don't ever count on having both at once.

Place your clothes and weapons where you can find them in the dark.

An elephant: A mouse built to government specifications.

Courage is the complement to fear. A man who is fearless cannot be courageous. (He is also a fool.)

When the ship lifts, all bills are paid. No regrets. (The same as when the skids leave the ground.)

Rub her feet.

Never underestimate the power of stupidity.

Never frighten a little man. He will kill you. (Being a fairly small guy, I understand this one well.)

Expertise in one field does not carry over into other fields. But experts often think so. The narrower their field of knowledge, the more likely they are to think so.

Never try to out-stubborn a cat.

THE RULES: Old School F Company 1/160th SOAR

1. The truth changes
2. Don't ever separate people from their equipment
3. Shit happens
4. Don't let the train drive you
5. Don't do the crime if you can't do the time
6. Bad news doesn't get better with time
7. If you shoot yourself in the foot, don't complain because it hurts
8. If you are the one making the rules, see rule # 7
9. 10% of the people never get the word
10. No animal runs faster than a scared animal
11. Quit before they go postal
12. Perception is reality
13. You can't underbid shabby maintenance
14. You can't please all of the people all of the time
15. The rules apply unless they are inconvenient, but check rule #7

The Warrant Officers of F 1/160 established these rules around the 1992-93-time frame. Still true today. Not sure what #10 had to do with anything.

My current van, a 1966 Ford Econoline, left side view. You can probably tell I'm a Pink Floyd fan.

Right side view

Rear view

AH-6 team in Iraq, also on the bottom left of the back of my van, and also my tattoo.

Agree

Told ya!

In October of 2022, I made the pilgrimage to Ft. Rucker to add my signature to MH-60L 288. 288 is a Somalia veteran having been hit with an RPG (rocket-propelled grenade) while at a hover with guys on the ropes. It is a great testimony to the pilots who maintained their hover until the guys were on the ground, then released the ropes and limped the aircraft to a soccer field for landing. 288 was the last Black Hawk I flew. As a note, Ft. Rucker has been renamed Ft. Novosel, one of several Army installations being renamed due to political correctness. Too bad.

No more Mother Rucker

On 27 October 2022, Pam and I attended the 40th +1 (40th canceled due to COVID) 160th Anniversary Ball in Nashville, Tennessee. This is a view of both sides of the 40th +1 coin.

T-shirt quilt made by my friend Joy.

Jon Barker Is Officer & Gentleman

One of the most popular movies in 1982, "An Officer and a Gentleman," explored the exciting, grueling and competitive lives of U. S. Navy Officers Flight School candidates.

Richard Gere played the lead as the young candidate whose sheer grit and determination made his dream to become a U. S. Naval Officer a reality.

These and other admirable qualities combined with the love and devotion of his lovely wife and daughter brought native Fleming Countian Jon Barker a similar victory.

Recently, the 26-year-old son of Mr. and Mrs. James Barker graduated from U. S. Army Flight School with the rank of Warrant Officer I (WOI). He is now a qualified Aero Scout helicopter pilot after 10 months of rigorous training in Ft. Rucker, Alabama.

Last week, this Gazette reporter talked with Jon and his wife Pam about his ten months' schooling for this prestigious position. "It was hard on all of us, but we helped each other," they said.

The first six weeks were called WOC/D (Warrant Officer Candidate Military Development), and as Pam readily admitted, "This made basic training seem like a picnic."

One of the officers who addressed the group told them, "You do in 10 months what West Point does in four years."

Jon was one of the sixty who began the training but only 40 made it through graduation. He and the other candidates lived in a barracks virtually shut off from everyone else. "They had to march everywhere and weren't allowed to speak to anyone. We, wives, were allowed to visit our husbands one hour each Wednesdays and Sundays till 3 p.m.," Pam explained.

And, most of that time was spent helping them study and polishing brass and shoes. Everything had to be done by regulation or demerits were given. The men even had to iron and put their underwear into a seven inch roll!

"They even had to clean the inside of their toothpaste cap with a toothbrush; everything was spic and span and in the proper place," Pam said. Also, during this time, Jon and Pam were appointed Social Leaders which meant they coordinated all social activities for the group.

After six weeks of endless inspections, studying and no candy or soft drinks, Jon graduated and moved onto the second phase into the 61st Company. This lasted 10 weeks and he was able to come home on weekends.

After two weeks training, the candidates began flying in a small helicopter, TH55 that, according to Pam, looked like "an orange tinker toy."

"When Jon made his first flight, he was on cloud nine for days," Pam noted. While he and the other men studied, the women learned to be officers' wives. "We were expected to attend luncheons, learn how to organize luncheons, give speeches, etc. And, I loved every minute of it," Pam said.

After completion of this phase a Junior Phase Party was held; it was organized by Jon and Pam. Then, Jon transferred onto 62nd Company for 16 weeks. He also got to move home!!

During this time, he learned to fly a UHIH Huey helicopter which was much different from the TH55. "The difference is like changing from a volkswagon to a cadillac," Jon noted.

Training included two week rotation using a helicopter similator and an actual aircraft,80 plus hours instrument flying and emergency procedures. Twelve candidates whose academic and flying records are the best are

chosen to fly the OH58 Aero Scout. This means about four times as much studying, but "it's definitely worth it," Jon said.

Other activities were 40 hours contact and combat skills, low level flying and flying as close to the ground as possible plus 15 hours of night flying.

Schooling cost for each pilot is estimated at $126,000! "But, these men are learning to fly $2 million equipment to defend our country. Looks like we can't afford not to train them," Pam said.

The graduation ceremonies lasted three days including a formal ball and the Officers Club which again, Jon and Pam; organized. The graduates received their wings and the wives received diplomas and "wings," also. "We worked right along with our husbands during their schooling," she said.

During the ceremonies, Jon and Pam had the distinction of sitting at the General's head table. "It was very exciting," Pam added. Also, attending the ceremonies from here were Pam's mother, Mrs. Jewel Claypoole, Jon's mother, Mrs. Loval Barker, Bonnie Stidom, Rhonda and Cara Coffey.

After spending the holidays here, they have left for their new home at Ft. Lewis, Washington.

Jon is a 1974 Fleming County High School graduate and has been with the U. S. Army seven years. He completed his basic training at Ft. Knox, spent 14 months in Germany as a tank commander, graduated from drill sergeant's school and was named Outstanding Drill Sergeant.

He and the former Pam Planck have one daughter, Kerry, "eight, going on nine" who has taken ballet and tap four years and baton lessons for two years.

Just like in the movie, the Barkers had a happy ending; their dream was fulfilled. We predict this is the first of many.

Article written for the Flemingsburg, Kentucky, newspaper soon after my flight school graduation. I don't remember who did the interview.

The author on the ramp at Kandahar, Afghanistan

The end…again…really.

Made in the USA
Monee, IL
14 September 2023

42740490R00177